Stacey —
   After you read this, Please
fill in the blanks.
                    Love,
                    Dad
                    3/17/03

NERVE CENTER

Other Titles of Interest from Brassey's

NERVE CENTER

Inside the White House Situation Room

MICHAEL K. BOHN

Brassey's, Inc.
Washington, D.C.

Library of Congress Cataloging-in-Publication Data

Bohn, Michael K.
   Nerve center : inside the White House Situation Room / Michael K. Bohn.—1st ed.
     p. cm.
   Includes bibliographical references and index.
   1. United States. White House Situation Room.   2. Presidents—United States—Staff.   3. National security—United States.   I. Title.
JK552 .B64   2003
973.92—dc21   2002014962

ISBN 1-57488-438-7 (alk. paper)

Printed in the United States of America on acid-free paper that meets the American National Standards Institute Z39-48 Standard.

Brassey's, Inc.
22841 Quicksilver Drive
Dulles, Virginia 20166

First Edition

10 9 8 7 6 5 4 3 2 1

To the men and women
of the
White House Situation Room

CONTENTS

ACRONYMS

AmCits	American citizens
AP	Associated Press
CDR	Commander
CIA	Central Intelligence Agency
CIB	Central Intelligence Bulletin
CINC	Commander-in-Chief
CINCSAC	Commander-in-Chief, Strategic Air Command
CMC	Crisis Management Center
CNO	Chief of Naval Operations
comms	Communications
DCI	Director, Central Intelligence
DEA	Drug Enforcement Administration
DIA	Defense Intelligence Agency
DoD	Department of Defense
EEOB	Eisenhower Executive Office Building
EOB	Executive Office Building
EOP	Executive Office of the President
EXCOM	Executive Committee of the National Security Council
FAA	Federal Aviation Administration
FEMA	Federal Emergency Management Agency
FBI	Federal Bureau of Investigation
FBIS	Foreign Broadcast Information Service
HOS	Head of state
HUMINT	Human Intelligence
JCS	Joint Chiefs of Staff

LAN	Local Area Network
LDX	Long Distance Xerox
MAC-V	Military Assistance Command-Vietnam
MEMCON	Memorandum of Conversation
MOLINK	Moscow Link
NASA	National Aeronautics and Space Administration
NATO	North Atlantic Treaty Organization
NEC	National Economic Council
NIMA	National Imagery and Mapping Agency
NMCC	National Military Commend Center
NOIWON	National Operations and Intelligence Watch Office Network
NPIC	National Photographic Interpretation Center
NRRC	Nuclear Risk Reduction Center
NSA	National Security Agency
NSC	National Security Council
NSPG	National Security Planning Group
NSOC	National SIGINT Operations Center
NVA	North Vietnam Army
OEOB	Old Executive Office Building
ONI	Office of Naval Intelligence
PDB	President's Daily Brief
PEOC	President's Emergency Operations Center
PLO	Palestine Liberation Organization
POTUS	President of the United States
PROFS	National Security Council e-mail system
SCC	Special Coordinating Committee
SDI	Strategic Defense Initiative
SDO	Senior Duty Officer
SIGINT	Signals Intelligence
SS-9	Soviet surface-to-surface missile, the ninth so designated
UPI	United Press International
USN	United States Navy

USSR	Union of Soviet Socialist Republics
WASHFAX	Washington Facsimile
WAOCCC	Washington Area Operations and Command Center Committee
WHCA	White House Communications Agency

PREFACE

As I scheduled interviews for this book, I decided to leave Dr. Condoleezza Rice, President George W. Bush's national security adviser, and her staff for last. Like all Americans, I did not anticipate the terrorist attacks of September 11, 2001. With America at war against terrorism, Dr. Rice and her staff did not have time to speak with me. I am told, however, the Situation Room has carried on, as they have under every other national crisis since 1961.

I wish to thank Sandy Doyle for her assistance in transforming an idea into a book and Rick Russell at Brassey's for his continuing assistance and encouragement. I am indebted to John Poindexter for his patient tutoring on future technologies that might influence the Situation Room, as well as for his imaginative ideas. John's Project Genoa at the Defense Advanced Research Projects Agency helped me think about the future Situation Room. Thanks also go to Tony Lake for his interest and help.

I am grateful to the many people at several presidential libraries administered by the National Archives and Records Administration: Jim Hall at the Kennedy Library, Regina Greenwell and Phil Scott at the Johnson Library, Nancy Mirshah at the Ford Library, Polly Nodine at the Carter Library, Steve Branch at the Reagan Library, and Mary Finch at the George Bush Library. Thanks are also due Kate Henderson at the Smithsonian Institute, Laura Sharp and Katherine Lam-

bert at Warner Bros., Kelli Grant at *Newsweek,* and Wally Mc-
Namee for help with photographs.

In addition, I wish to acknowledge the Enright family—
Angela, Michael, and Sean—for their help in identifying the
contribution made by Chuck Enright to the Situation Room.
Special thanks go to Joy Dell McCabe for her memories of
Gerry McCabe.

To all of the people who took the time to talk to me about
their experiences in the Situation Room, I send my thanks, especially to David McManis, Dennis Chapman, Jim Fazio, Neil
O'Leary, Paul LeBras, Kevin Cosgriff, and Elliot Powell, all former directors of the Situation Room. Thanks also to my wife,
Elin, for all her moral support and to Allen Benn and Steve
Pickard for appearing to be interested in the book's progress
during our weekly golf game.

Finally, and I speak for everyone who worked in the Situation Room during the Reagan and Bush administrations,
thanks to former President George H. W. Bush for being such
a caring and thoughtful person.

PROLOGUE

"Gayle, it's the SDO in the Situation Room. We've had two embassy bombings in Africa."

Gayle Smith, the senior director for African Affairs at the National Security Council, was used to being awakened at all hours by duty officers at the White House Situation Room, the President's intelligence and alert center. War in Rwanda, peace negotiations in Eritrea, and problems in Uganda had often kept her from a good night's sleep during the last three years of President Bill Clinton's administration. But this sounded bad. Her clock read 3:45 A.M.

"I'm awake," Smith said. "What do you know so far?"

"There have been explosions at our embassies in Kenya and Tanzania. State has no direct communications with the embassies; however, they have cell phone contact with people at each site. We have no information about casualties or the scope of damage, but CNN is trying to get cameras on the scene ASAP. We have called Dick Clarke, Sandy, Leon Fuerth, and Jim Steinberg. Anyone else?"

"No, that's the right list," said Smith. Clarke was the President's point man on terrorism on the National Security Council (NSC) staff, and these explosions were probably just that. Sandy was Samuel R. "Sandy" Berger, the President's national security adviser; both Smith and Clarke worked for Berger. Fuerth was Vice President Al Gore's national security adviser and Steinberg was Berger's deputy. Smith expected Berger to notify the President immediately.

"I will be there in an hour," Smith said, knowing full well that the Situation Room duty officers were already making calls to the State Department, the Central Intelligence Agency (CIA), and any other agency that might have further information about the blasts.

Berger indeed did call President Clinton in the predawn hours of August 7, 1998. As the rest of America awoke that summer day, the morning TV news shows carried video highlights of the destruction wrought by huge bombs at the U.S. embassies in Nairobi, Kenya, and Dar es Salaam, Tanzania. The explosions killed 257 people that day, including 12 American citizens, and injured 5,000.

In retrospect, the 1998 embassy bombings seem less significant when compared with the tragedies of September 11, 2001. Yet the events in Africa provided a window into the workings of the Situation Room during a crisis. The Situation Room's phone call to Gayle Smith started a whirlwind of activity at the White House that lasted for more than two weeks and stretched the Situation Room to its operational limits. Further, overlaid on this severe drain on the President's energy was the suffocating scandal involving Clinton and a young White House intern named Monica Lewinski.

═ ═ ═

Gayle Smith arrived at the White House at 5:30 A.M. and immediately asked the Situation Room duty officers to set up a secure video teleconference between the White House and key operations centers in town. She wanted to exchange information with CIA, the Federal Bureau of Investigation (FBI), Department of State, and the National Military Command Center (NMCC) at the Pentagon. She also wanted to start the coordination of search and rescue operations and initiate both survivor assistance plans and criminal investigations. Situation Room Director Kevin Cosgriff called in off-duty Situation Room personnel not only to help Smith, but also to screen incoming information, draft reports for the President and his staff, and coordinate hundreds of phone calls.

"We worked this nonstop for days," said Smith. "The duty officers called me twenty times a day with updates. The strain was immense, but the Sit Room took care of all the procedural things so I could concentrate on the coordination process. And they did it with such effortless ease. I love the Sit Room."

Situation Room Senior Duty Officer (SDO) Tony Campanella reported for his regular shift at 6:00 that August morning, and he recalls immediately arranging four presidential phone calls.

"The President wanted to talk with our ambassador in Nairobi and the chief of mission in Dar es Salaam, as well as the presidents of Kenya and Tanzania," said Campanella. "At first we couldn't contact Ambassador Prudence Bushnell in Nairobi, but finally got through on her cell phone when she was at a hospital visiting the injured. We had trouble connecting with Tanzanian President Mkapa because he was on vacation at Victoria Falls in Zimbabwe. Finally, we lined everybody up in a row, Ambassador Bushnell; John Lange, the charge d'affaires in Dar es Salaam; Kenyan President Moi; and Mkapa. President Clinton just stayed on the phone, talking to each in turn."

The conference room in the Situation Room was the scene of almost continual meetings for the next few days. The Principals Committee met repeatedly to assess the situation and coordinate U.S. actions, as it had in previous crises during the Clinton years. It included the heads of national security agencies and thus principal advisers to the President—Sandy Berger, Secretary of State Madeline Albright, Secretary of Defense William Cohen, Joint Chiefs Chairman General Hugh Shelton, Director of Central Intelligence George Tenet, Leon Fuerth, and others. The Deputies Committee, made up of the second in command from each agency plus Jim Steinberg, also met in the Situation Room to consider issues that that the principals might need to address. Bonnie Glick, another SDO, remembered that the days passed quickly, a blur of meetings, reports, updates, and hurried phone calls. Situation Room duty officers also arranged phone calls from President Clinton to the families of the slain Americans. Gayle Smith recalled that it was a difficult undertaking because of the confusion about identities, who was actually killed and who was injured.

President Clinton left Washington on August 10 for a fund-raising trip, but abruptly cancelled it late the next evening. He returned to Washington just before dawn on August 12 and met immediately with his national security team in the Situation Room. Confessions of several suspected terrorists detained by Pakistan shortly after the bombings suggested that the organization of the notorious terrorist Osama bin Laden was behind the bombings. Further, as the U.S. news media later revealed, intercepted mobile phone conversations also implicated bin Laden. Reportedly comfortable with the credibility of the evidence, Clinton left the Situation Room and walked to the Oval Office to meet with just a few advisers—the "Small Group"—to begin planning U.S. retaliation for the bombings. The President wanted to minimize the number of people involved in the planning of military operations in an attempt to catch bin Laden off-guard. Even the Situation Room duty officers were kept out of the planning until just prior to the retaliatory strikes.

On August 13, Clinton honored the Americans killed in the Nairobi embassy in a memorial ceremony at Andrews Air Force Base just outside Washington, D.C. The next day, he met with the Small Group in the Oval Office. Clinton approved in principle military strikes in what became known as Operation Infinite Reach. The planners selected two targets, a bin Laden terrorist training camp south of Kabul, Afghanistan, and a factory in Khartoum, Sudan, that officials believed, at that time, manufactured an ingredient for a deadly nerve gas. Planners set the attack for August 20 because they thought that terrorists had scheduled a convention of sorts for that date at the Afghan target.

Monday, August 17, was a tough day for President Clinton. He met with his national security advisers in the solarium on the third floor of the White House. Then, in the White House Map Room, he testified, via closed circuit TV, before a grand jury empaneled to examine his alleged affair with Monica Lewinski. Later that evening, before a nationwide television audience, he admitted having misled judicial authorities and the American public about his relationship with the former White House intern.

President Clinton and his family departed Washington for a vacation on Martha's Vineyard on August 18 amid wild news media speculation about the state of the Clintons' marriage. Kevin Cosgriff, who often traveled with the President on domestic trips to serve as liaison between Sandy Berger and the President, joined them. "It was a difficult trip under trying circumstances," said Cosgriff. "There were a lot of phone calls between the President and Mr. Berger, with the President always asking if there was any new intelligence."

At 3:00 A.M. on August 20, Clinton gave Berger the go-ahead for the strikes. U.S. Navy ships and submarines proceeded to launch seventy cruise missiles into Afghanistan and six at the Sudan target. Clinton announced the attack to the news media that afternoon at an elementary school gym on Martha's Vineyard, then flew back to Washington to address the nation on TV to explain the strikes. He returned to his island retreat the next day, amid cries from some critics that he deflected attention from his scandalous behavior with military action. Many critics even compared Clinton's actions with the story line in a popular film at the time, *Wag the Dog*, in which presidential advisers fake a war to divert attention from a presidential sex scandal.

The Situation Room staff carefully watched for potential terrorist reactions to the cruise missile attacks. Many believe that the destruction of Pan Am Flight 103 over Lockerbie, Scotland, in 1988 was an act of revenge for the 1986 U.S. attack on Libya, itself retaliation for a terrorist bombing in Berlin. On August 25, an explosion at a Planet Hollywood restaurant in Capetown, South Africa, caught the Situation Room's interest and, worse, a SwissAir MD-11 airliner fell out of the sky over the North Atlantic on September 2. Situation Room Duty Officer Tony Campanella remembered giving close scrutiny to the SwissAir accident because of the potential parallel to the Lockerbie incident. Nevertheless, no one connected either the restaurant bombing or the aircraft accident to the U.S. retaliatory strikes.

Titillating sexual scandals notwithstanding, all of this was business as usual for the Situation Room. Whether it was handling initial notifications of the bombings, following up with crisis reporting, arranging for presidential phone calls, hosting interagency coordination meetings, or supporting a beleaguered President on vacation, the Situation Room kept its energy focused on the job at hand.

1

IT'S NOT JUST
A ROOM

The White House Situation Room is not an underground command center where the news media, TV shows, and films often portray the President "huddling with his advisers" during crises. First, while technically in the basement of the West Wing of the White House, Situation Room duty officers look out large, ground-floor windows onto a spot of lawn between the West Wing and the Eisenhower Executive Office Building. Each spring, the U.S. Park Service plants red geraniums in window boxes outside the Situation Room.

Second, the Situation Room is actually a collection of rooms and its personnel perform a variety of functions for the President and his staff. There is the oft-mentioned conference room, the site of myriad meetings over the years, with or without the President, in crisis or not. There is also a watch center where teams of duty officers monitor a river of information about worldwide events, alerting the President, Vice President, and White House staff of breaking news, both of international and major domestic significance. The Situation Room is also part of a communications center that links the White House to the world. In addition, Situation Room duty officers and analysts write summaries of important events and help funnel the flow of reporting to the President from national security agencies such as CIA, State Department ("State"), and the Pentagon. The Situation Room is also the White House Help Desk. The duty officers are beacons of light for a weary staffer on a dark, troubled night, and a friendly, yet professional voice on the telephone. The Situation Room is not quite what the movies make it out to be, but, in many ways, much, much more.

McGeorge Bundy, President Kennedy's national security adviser, created the Situation Room in May 1961. While Bundy and his deputy, Walt Rostow, discussed the need for a message center in the White House in first few weeks of the administration, the concept gained momentum for several reasons, two of which stand out—Kennedy's attention to detail and his use of the NSC staff.

Kennedy read voraciously and absorbed huge amounts of information. He preferred written briefings to oral presentations and summaries of events, and he wanted the raw information from the field, information he couldn't get unless the State Department, the Pentagon, and CIA sent the White House individual cables and intelligence reports. The disastrous Bay of Pigs operation, a CIA-backed invasion of Cuba in 1961, convinced Kennedy's staff that they needed a communications facility at the White House to receive, sort, and distribute those cables.

According to Arthur Scheslinger, an adviser to President Kennedy, the Bay of Pigs failure also taught Kennedy that he needed more than just the advice from the experts at the vast Defense, State, and intelligence bureaucracies. Scheslinger wrote in his book, A Thousand Days, that Kennedy wanted his closest advisers, people like Ted Sorensen and Kennedy's brother Bobby, to help him make decisions regardless of their specialties or experience in international affairs. He wanted his national security adviser—Bundy—to be a personal, presidential adviser. Previously, the person with that title had been an aide to the National Security Council during the Truman and Eisenhower years, not a presidential adviser. Further, in order for his White House advisers to be active and effective, they needed access to the same information, at the same time, as the bureaucratic experts and Cabinet secretaries. From these two forces—a detail-oriented President and an activist White House staff loyal only to the President—sprang the White House Situation Room.

In 1961, during the scant weeks between the April 19 defeat of the invasion force of Cuban exiles at the Bay of Pigs and May 15, Kennedy's naval aide, Commander Tazewell Shepard, built the Situation Room. He and Bundy selected a space in the West Wing basement and Shepard employed Navy Seabees (sailors from the Construction Battalion) and a private contractor to transform West Wing spaces into a facility that some political scientists say changed the fundamental nature of the presidency.

Alert Center

The White House Situation Room is, first and foremost, the President's alert center. Situation Room duty officers, working twenty-four hours a day, seven days a week, monitor information about wars, terrorism, natural disasters, and other "situations" that impact on the national security of the United States. Important sources of such information have been, and continue to be, reporting from U.S. embassies abroad, military commands, intelligence agencies, and the news media. In recent years, however, cable TV news channels and the Internet have become, in many instances, the preeminent sources of information on fast-breaking events.

The year 1961 was just a few years removed from the time when couriers carried news of breaking international events by hand to the White House. Men in striped pants used to walk across the street between the White House and the State, War, and Navy Building (later the Eisenhower Executive Office Building) with cables and reports in their briefcases. When the Pentagon was built during World War II and the State Department moved four blocks west to Foggy Bottom in the 1950s, the men got in their cars to carry information to the White House. Luckily, the pace of crises in those days about equaled the speed of a '49 Ford.

Since then, not only has the speed of communications increased, but also the speed at which governments gather and transmit relevant information. The Situation Room receives thousands of electronic cables and messages each day. Most are from overseas embassies, CIA field stations, other intelligence agencies such as the Defense Intelligence Agency (DIA) and the National Security Agency (NSA), and the military services. Most of the communications are important but relatively routine, reports of global military, political, scientific, and economic developments. Interspersed is the infrequent "FLASH" message announcing a breaking event.

The Situation Room staff also monitors the news media for information on international events. Early on, that meant watching network television, reading national newspapers, and scanning reports filed by several news wire services. Today, the onrush of information generated by cable news channels—CNN, MSNBC, and Fox—and the Internet often overwhelm those traditional sources.

The duty officers screen the incoming information with the help of computers, looking for things that pass a series of escalating thresholds. By way of illustration, I've used a hypothetical scenario of escalating Israeli–Palestinian tensions.

- *Data of interest to NSC staff members*—The Israeli government huffs and puffs at the Palestinians.

- *Information that the President's national security adviser should see*—Reports that the Israelis might bomb Palestinian targets.
- *Things the President should know immediately*—Israeli planes bomb Palestinian offices with a high casualty rate.

These relatively young professionals have become adept over the years in knowing whom to wake up and when, and they rarely convey good news. "If the phone rang at 2:00 in the morning, it had to be either the President or the Situation Room," said Anthony Lake, President Clinton's first national security adviser. "Either way, my night was usually shot."

Other alert centers in Washington do the same thing for their respective bosses. The Pentagon has the National Military Command Center and the State Department, CIA, NSA, and Treasury all have operations centers. Each military service has command and intelligence centers. There is some duplication of effort among these centers, but there is an overarching, cardinal rule in Washington's indication and warning circles that ensures some duplication—"Don't let your boss be the last to know." If something threatens American interests abroad, all agencies work hard to ensure that a high-ranking colleague does not surprise their respective bosses. If the President's national security adviser calls an unknowing secretary of state and surprises him with the question, "What do you think about the Lima situation?," heads will roll at State's Operations Center.

Bob O'Hara, an analyst from NSA who worked under both Reagan and George H. W. Bush, recalled an instance when the Situation Room had to alert and brief all of the agency heads as well as the national security adviser.

"There was a coup attempt in Panama against Manuel Noriega, and it could not have happened on a worse day," said O'Hara. "The president of Mexico was in Washington on a

state visit and that morning President Bush and all of his national security advisers were on the South Lawn at a ceremony
welcoming President Carlos Salinas to the White House. I had
to intercept Bush's national security adviser, Brent Scowcroft,
and Secretary of State James Baker as they reentered the
White House (with their Mexican counterparts). I pulled them
aside and briefed them on the events in Panama, and near
chaos broke out."

O'Hara said that the U.S. hosts and the Mexican delegation
moved immediately into high-level meetings in the Roosevelt
and Cabinet rooms. The U.S. officials were unwilling to share
news on the Noriega coup with the Mexicans at that point, but
all the principals still wanted updates. "All of the Cabinet officers were disconnected from their watch centers, so the Sit
Room tried hard to keep everyone informed about the situation," O'Hara continued. "The director designated me as the
conduit and I pulled Scowcroft and Gates [Scowcroft's deputy,
Robert Gates] out of the Cabinet room, briefed them, then did
the same with Baker throughout the morning. I spent more
time in Patty Presock's office [President Bush's secretary] and
the Oval Office that day than during my entire tenure at the
White House."

Communications

Second, the Situation Room is an integral part of the White
House communications system. The White House Communications Agency (WHCA), a military unit, actually provides and
operates the most of communications systems, twists the wires
together, and connects the White House to the rest of the
world. But WHCA (referred to as "WHAKKA" at 1600 Pennsylvania Avenue) is the generally unseen, underwater portion of
the iceberg that represents the White House communications

world. The Situation Room is the tip of the iceberg and helps the President, his White House advisers, and the NSC staff take advantage of a variety of cable, fax, voice, and video tele-communications systems that WHCA provides. If WHCA were a bank, the Sit Room would be the teller window.

When Bundy and Shepard built the Situation Room, they preempted several wartime reserve communications circuits and devices in the basement of the East Wing of the White House. Military technicians quickly connected them into the communications networks controlled by CIA, State, and the Defense Department ("Defense").

At first, communications technicians hand-carried the in-coming cables to and from the East Wing to the Situation Room in the West Wing, but later WHCA added pneumatic tubes to speed the process. Gradually, WHCA replaced the mechanical teletypes with computers that processed the traf-fic, but the Situation Room duty officers or the NSC Secretar-iat had to distribute printed copies of the cables throughout the NSC staff and White House. The Reagan administration ushered in soft copy or electronic distribution, not only of clas-sified cables, but also incoming news stories. Today, the Situa-tion Room even distributes video streams to NSC and White House staff members via an individual's desktop monitor.

The Kennedy administration began the continually evolving process of installing specialized communications systems. They added direct telephone lines to President Charles de Gaulle of France, Britain's Prime Minister Harold Macmillan, German Chancellor Conrad Adenauer, and others. The Situa-tion Room called the circuit to Great Britain the "Mac-Jack" line in honor of Jack Kennedy and Harold Macmillan. Henry Kissinger, Nixon's national security adviser, also added select circuits, and President Carter's staff installed secure or enci-phered teleprinter systems over direct lines to the country's major allies and to Egypt.

Today, the Situation Room has, either on its own or through WHCA, access to the government's most sophisticated communications devices. They exchange cables with U.S. and many foreign government agencies and can talk to any U.S. government official and many foreign leaders on a secure (enciphered, or "scrambled") telephone. They transmit and receive both unclassified and secure faxes. And—with help from WHCA and the White House switchboard—they are able to connect the Situation Room to just about anyone in the world who has a phone, especially foreign heads of state.

== == ==

"Mr. President, this is Bonnie in the Situation Room. Prime Minister Blair has been delayed. Would you like to wait on the line 'til he picks up?"

Arranging international telephone calls for the President is one of the Situation Room's more demanding communications responsibilities. Bonnie Glick, senior duty officer during the late 1990s, remembered the Blair phone call as unusual because the other head of state normally comes on the line first. Since the President always initiates the call, protocol dictates that he comes on the line last. Also, President Clinton was often late to any appointment, thus making it doubly unusual for him to be on the line first. Glick described the situation:

"It was on a Sunday morning and the President was working the *Times* crossword puzzle while he waited for Blair. Suddenly he broke the silence and asked if anyone in the Sit Room knew of a college town in Maine. We had him on a speaker so one of my assistants, a Mainer, heard the clue and said, 'Tell the President it's Orono, O-R-O-N-O.' I passed that along to Mr. Clinton, who said, 'That's it!' and thanked us for the help."

Conference Room

The Situation Room complex contains a conference room in which the President occasionally meets with national security advisers. In some cases, the group is the formal National Security Council, the assembly created by law in 1947—the President, Vice President, and the Secretaries of State and Defense; the director of Central Intelligence and the Chairman of the Joint Chiefs of Staff were designated official advisers. (The director of the Central Intelligence Agency is also the titular head of the entire U.S. foreign intelligence community and thus normally uses the title of his larger job, director of Central Intelligence, or DCI.) More often, presidents add other, close advisers such as his chief of staff and the Attorney General to NSC meetings.

How much a President uses the conference room for meetings depends on his individual style of considering issues and making decisions. During the Cuban Missile Crisis, Kennedy met with the Executive Committee (EXCOM) of the NSC in the Cabinet Room or the Oval Office. Nixon and Ford almost never used the conference room; Nixon waited for a written summary of his advisers' recommendations. Principal advisers to George H. W. Bush and Clinton met regularly in the conference room, but those two presidents generally joined their national security teams later in the Cabinet Room, Oval Office, or the Mansion. Clinton usually met with his advisers in the Situation Room only when considering military actions.

During crises, Johnson met so often with his advisers in the Situation Room that he brought his chair down from the Oval Office. Reagan met several times each month in the Situation Room with a rump group of the NSC—the National Security Planning Group—to discuss pending decisions on national security matters and was comfortable there during crises. In 2001, President George W. Bush met in the Situation Room daily at 9:30 A.M. during the planning for military operations in Afghanistan and also after the air campaign began. If one of Bush's principals could not attend, he joined the group via video teleconferencing, a technological advance that has virtually expanded the conference room since the late 1980s.

The conference room is only about eighteen feet square, and Henry Kissinger described the room in his memoir, *White House Years*, as "uncomfortable, unaesthetic and essentially oppressive." Its dimensions have remained mostly unchanged since its construction in 1961. In the center stands a polished wooden table that seats ten in comfortable leather chairs, but it leaves little room for much else. There are smaller chairs along the walls, often seating the seconds to the principals at the table, and the polished cherry paneling hides only large TV monitors, not huge, complex displays and flashing lights. There are a few telephones in the room, one even built into the table by the President's chair during Reagan's time, but people rarely use them. The President uses the conference room to meet with his advisers, not to push buttons, call Moscow on the phone, or launch missiles. If the President makes a decision, usually the advisers get in their limousines, go back to their own high-tech command centers, and make things happen.

But this small conference room has captured the imagination of the entertainment industry. In the film *Air Force One*, the President, played by Harrison Ford, valiantly resists hijackers of his aircraft. On the ground, the Vice President, Secretary of Defense, and the joint chiefs organize rescue attempts in the Situation Room. In the film, the room is large, tastefully decorated, and filled with TV monitors, computers, and attentive staff. The on-screen complex appears to be about the size of a basketball court.

Why then does the entertainment industry create versions of the space that are far grander than the actual room, with electronic displays and maps of the world? "Dramatic effect," said Ken Hardy, production designer for NBC's weekly TV drama, *The West Wing*. "We used some photos of the conference room from President Johnson's time to create the set, but we thought a larger and darker environment lent more gravity to the story lines. We wanted the room to match the image, the icon that it has become, rather than reality." Hardy and other cast and crew members from the show toured the Situation Room during a visit to the White House in 2000, but he said they didn't want to change the set at that point.

The dark, TV version of the Situation Room caught the eye of Condoleezza Rice, President Bush's national security adviser during the summer of 2001. *U.S. News and World Report* quoted her reaction to the TV show. "The rooms [the real Sit Room spaces] are well lit. They are not particularly well air conditioned because we are trying to save energy." She also told reporters in late October 2001 that meetings in the Sit Room with President Bush about the war in Afghanistan were not like movie scenes in which the actors examine maps. The White House termed the meetings "businesslike" with structured agenda.

I asked former President Bush about his reaction to *The West Wing* portrayal of the conference room, and he said, "I don't watch *West Wing*, so I have not seen their version."

Why hasn't the facility grown like everything else in the government?

The answer is that real estate in the White House is too dear. An office in the West Wing is the most desirable badge of power available to the staff because proximity to the Oval Office translates into influence. No one will give up that valuable space to enlarge the Situation Room.

Early in the Reagan administration, the President's advisers wanted a bigger, more robust facility. They converted what had been the secretary of state's office during World War II in the Old Executive Office Building into large, new facility—the Crisis Management Center. Full of the requisite bells and whistles, the room was a technological marvel. But soon, no senior staffers went there during crises because it was across the street. Everyone went to the Situation Room because it's just downstairs from the Oval Office and people were used to dealing with the Situation Room staff. Although no longer called the Crisis Management Center, the room is still configured to serve as a crisis meeting room.

The White House staff often uses the conference room for other, more mundane meetings. Clinton's national security advisers, Tony Lake, Sandy Berger (both avid baseball fans), and others used the conference room to conduct their Rotisserie League draft during Clinton's first term. Rotisserie League members select real baseball players for fantasy teams that compete using the performance of the real players to determine the outcome of games between the make-believe teams. Tony Lake recalled their hobby: "We held our player drafts in the Situation Room, each of us chipping in twenty-three dollars to build a pot that went to the winning team at the end of the season. But I heard about some federal employees at the Department of Commerce who got in trouble for gambling on government property for doing the same thing. Sandy and I quickly stopped using the Sit Room for Rotisserie League business."

Reporting

The Situation Room staff writes reports of significant activity, both in summary and short, timely notes, for distribution in the White House. The recipients vary during each administration, but the Situation Room generally sends its reports to the President, Vice President, the President's chief of staff and national security adviser, NSC staff members, and other, selected White House staff.

Situation Room duty officers began writing a summary of

overnight activities during the Cuban Missile Crisis, a tense confrontation in 1962 between the U.S. and the Soviet Union about Soviet deployment of offensive missiles in Cuba. The report contained not only brief overviews of incoming cables, but also descriptions of events within the White House. Bundy pressed one of his assistants, Michael Forrestal, into duty as a supplementary watch stander during those thirteen tense days in October 1962. He made the following entries in his summary of October 24:

> 8:30 P.M. *Copy of the message from JCS (6917) was received ordering CINCSAC to start "Generation of Forces." CDR Mc-Cabe suggested the President be made aware of this, and after checking with Gilpatric, I informed the President, who approved, after having been told that McNamara and Gilpatric had approved.* [Note: JCS was Joint Chiefs of Staff and 6917 was the message serial number; CINCSAC was Commander-in-Chief Strategic Air Command; Lieutenant Commander Gerry McCabe was an assistant to Kennedy's naval aide; Robert McNamara was Secretary of Defense, and Roswell Gilpatric was his deputy. The cable directed strategic forces to increase their readiness to Defense Condition 2 and prepare for possible war.]

> 9:30 P.M. *Report from Harlan Cleveland on events in the United Nations. Zorin's statement after Adlai's did not deny presence of missiles in Cuba, but did deny offensive purposes. An* [sic] *UAR-Algerian draft resolution has been prepared asking for a freeze of all action and a return to the status quo ante October 22.* [Note: Cleveland was Assistant Secretary of State for International Organizational Affairs; V. A. Zorin was the Soviet Ambassador to the United Nations (UN) who, when confronted with aerial photographs of Soviet ballistic missiles in Cuba, obfuscated and made blustery denials. Adlai Stevenson, the U.S. Ambassador to the UN, angrily confronted Zorin during a meeting of the UN Security Council. UAR was the United Arab Republic, a short-lived union between Egypt and Syria.]

> 10:30 *P.M.* *The President was interested in whether Zorin denied the presence of missiles in Cuba. David Ormsby Gore had told him that Zorin had made such a denial. My information from Cleveland was to the contrary and presidential ire mounted from the conflict of information, and that no one in this government had the text of Zorin's statement.* [*Note:* Ormsby Gore was the U.K. Ambassador to the U.S.]

The Situation Room daily summary has continued since 1962, the staff adapting the content and format to the needs of the national security adviser and the President. Johnson demanded detailed accounts of the fighting in Vietnam, and the staff skewed the summary in that direction. Brent Scowcroft, President Ford's national security adviser, wanted summaries of top newspaper stories included. Late in the Reagan administration, the staff reproduced the twice-daily summary (6:00 A.M. and 6:00 P.M.) on blue paper, and it became known as the "Blue Thing" throughout the White House. When President Clinton traveled, the Situation Room changed the distribution times to match morning and evening times in whatever time zone in which he was located.

The Situation Room, acting on behalf of the national security adviser to the President, has helped funnel daily reporting from Cabinet agencies to the President. Paramount among those routine reports is the CIA's *President's Daily Brief* (PDB), which the agency has sent to presidents for almost forty years. In some administrations, CIA sent the PDB to the Situation Room for distribution in the White House; in others CIA delivered it directly to either the President or his national security adviser. Also, each President adopted different approaches to what McGeorge Bundy described to John Kennedy as "his daily dozen." Some presidents welcomed both the briefers and the PDB; others opted for either the PDB or oral briefs. President Clinton initially accepted both the PDB and the briefers, but soon began canceling the briefings, reportedly because travel and the demands of his domestic agenda distracted him. Jim Woolsey, Clinton's first director of Central Intelligence, had originally accompanied the briefers to the White House, but as their appointments were repeatedly cancelled, he stopped showing up. Retired Admiral Bill Studeman was Woolsey's deputy at the start of the Clinton presidency and recalled Woolsey's frustration in Clinton's initial disinterest in intelligence matters: "Some crazy crashed his single-engine plane onto the south grounds of the White House in 1994 and the word around the intelligence community was that the pilot was really Jim Woolsey, trying to get an appointment with President Clinton."

Personnel

The size and composition of the Situation staff has fluctuated over the years since its inception. Initially, a lone CIA intelligence analyst worked a twenty-four-hour shift in the Situation Room, sleeping on a cot there during the night. Military communications technicians from the White House Communications Agency and assistants to the President's naval aide supported the duty officer. For much of the time since the 1970s, three duty officers and a communications assistant have been on watch around the clock. By 1985, the duty officers were organized into five teams, each team standing a series of twelve-hour shifts from 6:00 A.M. to 6:00 P.M., a series of twelve-hour night shifts, then a string of normal, eight-hour days from Monday through Friday. After a break, they repeated the cycle.

Today, one duty officer generally processes incoming news reports and a second screens electrical messages from the intelligence community, State and Defense Departments, and other government agencies. A third is the senior duty officer for that shift and supervises the team. WHCA provides the communications technicians.

Two intelligence analysts, or "day workers," assist the duty officers in the Situation Room. They generally work Monday through Saturday morning, one starting about midnight, the second around 7:00 A.M. Both assist in the preparation of Situation Room reports and, during crises, help coordinate Situation Room activities in support of the crisis managers. It is important to note that the Situation Room staff does not manage crises at the White House, but rather they help those who do—people such as the national security adviser and NSC staff members who have specific regional and functional responsibilities.

Government agencies in the national security business—CIA, State, Defense, Defense Intelligence Agency, military intelligence services, NSA, and the Coast Guard—loan personnel to the White House to fill the Situation Room staff positions, normally for one- or two-year assignments. Civilians are usually GS-9 through GS-13 (federal civil service grades), and the military officers are usually O3 (Army captain, Navy lieutenant) through O4 (Army major and Navy lieutenant commander). Situation Room tours of duty are tremendously career-enhancing for these relatively junior people. If they arrive with generally narrow views of international affairs and the intelligence world, they leave with a vastly enlarged horizon. They quickly become knowledgeable about virtually everything important to the national security of their country.

In recent years, the Situation Room Director has been a military officer. Prior to 1985, Situation Room directors were drawn from CIA, NSA, or State. I was the first military director since 1963, and a series of officers from the Air Force, Army, and Navy followed me. There were two exceptions—a civilian from DIA, Neil O'Leary, and the first woman director, Joyce Harmon from CIA.

The short tours of duty and the relatively junior grade of the duty officers create a demanding training and indoctrination environment for the director and his deputy. The contributing agencies take care to send their best candidates, and the vast majority of personnel assigned to the Situation Room have been extraordinarily competent and have exercised sound judgment. There have been, however, exceptions. In January 1987, I received a telephone call from CIA headquarters:

"Commander Bohn, one of our people assigned to the Situation Room is trying to sell shredded White House documents," a CIA security official exclaimed. "This is a serious security breach and I want to meet with you immediately."

Whoa. The document part was okay. The Situation Room's shredder—we called it the Alligator—was so effective that we were authorized to pitch the remains in the trash. The sales part, however, worried me.

Two CIA security officers came down from Langley that afternoon and were relieved to hear that classified documents were not compromised. But their tale about what led to their visit was an unusual one.

During the previous November, when the story of the Iran-Contra affair broke across the news media, Oliver ("Ollie") North and his secretary, Fawn Hall, frantically shredded incriminating documents in his office. When his shredder became overloaded, Ollie took some of the documents to the Situation Room to shred, and my CIA watch officer knew what he had seen. When Ollie left, the watch officer removed the plastic bag of remains—it looks like extremely fine, angel hair pasta—and took it home that night.

Within weeks, he tried to sell plastic pill bottles full of shredded Iran-Contra papers. "Authentic White House papers from Ollie North's safe! Only $2.95, two for $5.00!"

Help Desk

"It's an island of calm."

That's how Leon Fuerth, Vice President Al Gore's national security adviser for eight years, responded when asked to describe the Situation Room. He was, of course, referring to the aura projected by the people who staff the facility, not the conference room that is often the scene of frenetic meetings during crises. And it has been the young professionals who are responsible for that aura—they not only define the Situation Room's personality, they also make it a place where every White House staff member seeks help. They top the list of friendly and helpful offices in the White House. Apolitical and without guile, the Sit Room staff operates a 24/7 Help Desk for everyone in the Executive Office of the President. Fuerth knew this well.

"I was in Manhattan for a meeting and left the hotel to move my car," said Fuerth. "I quickly got lost and had no idea how to return to the hotel. I reached for my cell phone, called the Sit Room, and told them what corner I was standing on. They pulled up a map on their computer and gave me directions back to the hotel."

Chuck Enright, the first duty officer in the Situation Room, recalled in a 1986 letter a difficult request from President Kennedy in 1962.

"The naval aide called from Hyannis Port one Sunday evening at 10:00 and said the President wanted a copy of every *Time* and *Newsweek* magazine for the past year at his bedside in Hyannis Port when he got up in the morning," wrote Enright. "I groaned, phoned the librarian for the NSC, and she told me that she had only a few issues in her office but could get others from D.C. public libraries to which she had access at any time. I arranged for the copies to be put aboard the courier plane that left at 4:00 A.M., and the deadline was met."

More than just people needed help. Presidential pooches
King Timahoe (Nixon), Lucky (Reagan), and Buddy (Clinton)
were welcomed just as warmly as the Sit Room staff met their
masters. Buddy, a rambunctious chocolate Labrador Retriever,
seemed like a handful when the TV cameras caught him chas-
ing sticks on the South Lawn. Occasionally, that energy was
too much for the Oval Office, and Clinton's steward brought
him downstairs to the Situation Room. Like any other Lab,
Buddy had to touch someone when he sat or lay down and
often ended up under a computer console, sitting on a duty
officer's feet.

= = =

During the last days of President Carter's term, he and his staff
were desperately trying to arrange the release of the American
hostages seized at the American embassy in Tehran, Iran, the
year before. Carter, whose unsuccessful bid for reelection was
thought by many observers to have been partially caused by his
inability to end the prolonged hostage situation, came to the
Oval Office early each morning to review overnight developments in Tehran. To Carter's immense disappointment, Iran
held onto the hostages until he had left office.

In January 1981, just days before Carter left office and the inauguration of Ronald Reagan, an ice storm kept Carter's national security adviser, Zbigniew Brzezinski, from driving to the
White House. Brzezinski called Dennis Chapman, the director
of the Situation Room, asking him to gather the President's
daily intelligence reports together and take them to the Oval Office. Chapman told me of the touching moment that followed.

"I briefed the President on our morning take while he sat by
the fireplace," recalled Chapman. "He was tired and I saw the
effects of this long crisis on his face. Afterwards, he rose from
his chair and while we walked toward his desk, he put his arm
around my shoulders. 'You know, Dennis,' he said, 'I knew that
I could always rely on the Situation Room, and it never let me
down.'"

2

ORIGINS

JFK and the Bay of Pigs

President John F. Kennedy, resplendent in white tie and tails, danced gracefully, despite his bad back, with his wife, Jacqueline, in the East Room of the White House. Soon, their guests at the reception honoring members of Congress joined the attractive First Couple on the dance floor. On that April evening in 1961, just eighty-eight days into the New Frontier, Kennedy radiated confidence and charm. The first chapter of Camelot in Washington was unfolding. Yet at that same moment and unknown to virtually all of the dancers, the shock waves of a U.S. foreign policy disaster were rapidly enveloping the White House. The CIA-sponsored attempt to invade Cuba and overthrow the communist regime of Fidel Castro with a force of Cuban exiles had fared badly, and that evening they were on the verge of defeat. Reports of the fiasco at the landing site, the Bay of Pigs, were flowing into the White House in a harrowing crescendo while the President danced.

At midnight, Kennedy left the Mansion for the Oval Office, where Vice President Lyndon Johnson, Secretary of State Dean Rusk, Secretary of Defense Robert McNamara, Chairman of the Joint Chiefs General Lyman Lemnitzer, and the Chief of Naval Operations Admiral Arleigh Burke joined him. All, including the President, still wore their formal attire. Kennedy's national security adviser, McGeorge Bundy; Bundy's deputy, Walt Rostow; presidential aide Arthur Schlesinger; and CIA Deputy Director for Plans Richard Bissell joined the group. The President had been meeting all day with these and other advisers to consider discouraging reports of the operation, but the latest news indicated that the brigade of exiles was in extremis.

As he had earlier in the day, Kennedy rejected all proposals to intervene directly with U.S. forces to rescue the invasion force. Castro's troops, as well as the swamps ringing the Bay of Pigs, surrounded the brigade. Although Kennedy approved some half measures, the momentum of the crisis clearly turned from relief and reinforcement to extraction and damage control. The operation had failed. After nearly three hours, the session wound down, but several of Kennedy's advisers remained, talking with the President. According to Peter Wyden in his book *Bay of Pigs*, Kenneth O'Donnell, Kennedy's appointments secretary and intimate, said that he had "never seen him [Kennedy] so distraught."

The White House Situation Room grew out of the Bay of Pigs disaster. No one remembers an electric moment when Bundy or Rostow said, "We could have avoided that fiasco if only we had a crisis center in the White House." Rather, the incident appeared to have been a catalyst that unified disparate forces already at work in the nascent Kennedy administration.

Mainly, Kennedy wanted more details about international events than the national security apparatus was accustomed to providing his predecessor, Dwight D. Eisenhower. His early, oral intelligence briefings, which he considered too general, displeased him. He also absorbed written reports faster than a briefer talked because his reading speed was so high. According to Kennedy's military assistant, Major General Chester V. "Ted" Clifton, the new President preferred primary source documents, not summaries of events. He wanted the actual cable from one of his ambassadors, not a State Department summary. He asked for specific CIA intelligence reports, not one-paragraph references in a daily intelligence brief.

CIA did not provide President Kennedy with many of the operational details during the Bay of Pigs operation. The selection of the invasion landing site was an example. Arthur Schlesinger wrote in A *Thousand Days* that Kennedy thought that the original CIA plan for a large amphibious landing at the coastal city of Trinidad was "too spectacular." Accordingly, CIA selected as an alternative the Bay of Pigs, about 100 miles to the west of Trinidad, even though swamps surrounded the bay. Walt Rostow described how that detail—a change the landing area—influenced the President's thinking. "When CIA changed the site, the impact of the shift didn't filter up to the President, "Rostow said. "Earlier, the planners told Kennedy that if the invasion failed, the exiles would escape into the mountains north of Trinidad and undertake guerrilla operations against Castro. Later, as defeat of the invasion force seemed imminent, we expected the survivors to flee to the hills. They did not because of the swamps surrounding the bay. Had Kennedy known the details of the landing site change, he might have made different decisions."

The Bay of Pigs disaster also convinced Kennedy and Bundy that they must have the same facts that the bureaucracies of State, CIA, and Defense had used for their individual, institutional analysis and interpretation of national security matters. The White House staff's knowledge of the fundamental facts underlying issues could be used to, in the words of Schlesinger, "make impolite inquiry and the rude comment," ask the right questions, and evaluate the answers. The best way to get the facts was to get the cables that U.S. embassies abroad sent to the State Department, messages that U.S. military commands sent to the Pentagon, and the intelligence reports that collectors sent to CIA headquarters—in other words, set up a communications center at the White House. The President's staff then received the same raw information that the national security bureaucracy received and at the same time. While critics said this communications capability would allow the President's staff to second-guess Cabinet officials, Kennedy's advisers saw it as a means to prevent future disasters like the Bay of Pigs operation.

The second impact the Bay of Pigs disaster had on the creation of a White House crisis center was on the roles of President Kennedy's White House staff. Kennedy, according to Schlesinger, set about to use his personal staff differently from the way his predecessors had, to ensure that he suffered no more incidents like the Bay of Pigs. Schlesinger continued: "The first lesson was never to rely on the experts. He now knew he had to broaden the range of his advice, make greater use of the generalists in whom he had personal confidence and remake every great decision in his own terms. . . ."

The President henceforth relied heavily on the advice of his most trusted advisers. He wanted to hear from people like Bobby Kennedy, the attorney general, and Ted Sorensen, his special counsel and speechwriter, regardless of their nominal responsibilities and assignments. He recruited retired Army General Maxwell Taylor to be his White House adviser on military affairs. Further, Kennedy immediately put Bundy in charge of coordinating national security affairs in the White House.

Bundy also moved his office. He had inherited the spacious, but relatively remote, office in the Executive Office Building his predecessor had occupied in the Eisenhower administration. But just as it is today, a presidential adviser's influence with the boss is directly proportional to the adviser's distance from the Oval Office. When in his EOB office, Bundy often missed hastily called meetings with the President. Walt Rostow said the President told Bundy to "get your ass into the White House."

There was also the problem of relaying time-sensitive decisions made at the White House to the rest of the government for execution and action. President Kennedy's naval aide, Commander Tazewell Shepard, now a retired rear admiral, recalled the situation during the Bay of Pigs invasion:

"Kennedy met with everyone, including Secretary McNamara, Admiral Burke, and General Lemnitzer, in the Cabinet Room," said Shepard. "I sat outside during the meetings. If the President decided to reposition U.S. forces, Admiral Burke stuck his head out the door and passed the orders on to me. I then called the Joint Chiefs staff and relayed the President's instructions. After the incident was over, I told the President and Mac Bundy that the arrangement was unsatisfactory and that we should have a watch center in the White House."

The invasion of Cuba at the Bay of Pigs commenced on April 17, 1961. In the early morning hours of April 19, President Kennedy realized that the operation was not only a failure, but also an embarrassment to both him and the U.S. By mid-May, Mac Bundy and Taz Shepard had the White House Situation Room up and running in the West Wing.

≡ ≡ ≡

The creation of an intelligence and communications watch center in the White House in the spring of 1961 should have seemed, in hindsight, a long overdue event. In view of the Situation Room's immediate and enduring relevance to presidential activities since its inception, why wasn't there one before? Well, there was, actually—several, in fact.

During the Civil War, the War Department, located in a building adjacent to the White House at the site of the current

Eisenhower Executive Office Building, maintained a telegraph office. President Lincoln frequently visited the office to read reports of the fighting. President McKinley established a war room on the second floor of the Mansion during the Spanish-American War in 1898, but his staff abandoned the facility after the war.

The next watch center at the White House was President Franklin D. Roosevelt's Map Room during World War II. The Navy assigned George M. Elsey, a Reserve ensign at the time, to the Map Room and he described its operation in a 1964 oral history for the Truman Presidential Library. Elsey said that the White House established the Map Room shortly after Pearl Harbor on the ground floor of the White House, in the Mansion, not the West Wing. Army and Navy officers maintained maps and charts that depicted combat around the world. Captain John L. McCrea, FDR's naval aide at the outbreak of the war, supervised the activities of the Map Room. Rear Admiral Wilson Brown succeeded McCrea in 1943.

"The job of those of us—Map Room watch officers—was to maintain a twenty-four hour a day, seven day a week active room where telegrams and dispatches were received from the Army and the Navy," Elsey said in his oral history. "We were to transcribe the information onto maps and maintain current files, so that whenever the President or Mr. Hopkins (FDR's adviser) or Admiral William D. Leahy, the President's Chief of Staff, wanted to know what was going on we had the information instantly available for them."

Elsey also said that the Map Room acted as a center for classified communications. They encoded messages sent to Roosevelt when he traveled beyond the White House, as well as messages that FDR sent to Winston Churchill in Great Britain and Josef Stalin in the Soviet Union.

Captain McCrea created the Map Room by converting a ladies cloakroom next to the Diplomatic Reception Room on the ground floor of the Mansion. Elsey and his colleagues kept track of Allied and enemy troop movements with grease pencils on plastic sheets overlaid on National Geographic Society maps. They integrated into those plots information gained from decoded MAGIC and ULTRA intercepts of German and Japanese radio traffic. In a *National Geographic Magazine* article from 1995, Elsey wrote that Roosevelt visited the Map Room in the morning en route to the Oval Office from the family quarters, then on the return trip in the afternoon. "We pushed the wheelchair first to the main desk, where the latest war news—or possibly the latest message from Churchill—awaited in a black leather folder with 'The President' stamped in gold leaf on the front. Then we made a slow tour of the room. . . . Furniture was clustered in the center, leaving aisles on the four sides so FDR could study the maps at close range."

Upon Roosevelt's death, Truman continued to use the Map Room, especially as he prepared for the Potsdam Conference with his British and Soviet counterparts near the end of the war. The White House ceased the watch operations in the Map Room at war's end. Elsey saved one of the wartime maps, complete with plastic overlay and grease pencil annotations, and he said that it hangs today in what is still known as the Map Room.

=== === ===

In April 1961, Bromley Smith, a Foreign Service Officer seconded to the National Security Council from the State Department, was the executive secretary of the NSC. He and his boss, McGeorge Bundy, looked for a place to build the Situation Room, finally deciding to convert a bowling alley in the West Wing basement. They turned to Tazewell Shepard, JFK's naval aide, for help in constructing the facility.

"I had funds available in the Emergency Planning budget to

pay a contractor to begin work," Shepard said forty years later. "I also brought in some Seabees through the group that worked for me at Camp David. They worked at night on the conversion in order to keep from disturbing people working in adjacent offices, yet get the job done quickly."

The initial configuration of what was initially called the International Situation Room included four rooms—a conference room, a file room that was also a rear-projection booth for the conference room, a watch-standing station, and an office. Only the conference room remains today in its original location and size. The other rooms grew and changed in configuration over the succeeding years. The White House dropped the term "International" later.

The heart of the Situation Room, not only in 1961, but also throughout its history, was the communications system that produced the cables that President Kennedy and his staff wanted to read. At first, however, the lash-up was a rudimentary affair. In April 1961 there were teletype circuits that terminated in an old bomb shelter in the East Wing basement. The teletypes, which were little more than old, manual typewriters connected by communications circuits, had been installed for backup use in case of war, but Smith and Shepard usurped them for use by the new Situation Room. They arranged to connect the teletypes to the State, Defense, and CIA communications systems, as well as to the NSA. As mentioned earlier, at first, military communications technicians pulled incoming cables off the teletype printers and hand-carried them to the Situation Room in the West Wing. A few years later, engineers built pneumatic tubes to carry cables to the Situation Room. Eventually, WHCA, the military unit that has supported the Situation Room from the beginning, replaced the teletypes with the first of a series of computer systems that have processed incoming and outgoing cables with ever-increasing sophistication.

With the basic communications circuits in place, Bromley Smith began the tricky and politically charged process of persuading the national security agencies—State, Defense, the individual services, and CIA—into relaying cables to the White House. Two problems arose: First, the institutions proved reluctant to pass on raw information to a potentially second-guessing White House staff, especially information that they felt it was their duty to sift and sort, often at a maddeningly slow rate. Second, once Smith convinced the agencies that Kennedy really wanted this done, the agencies had to decide how much traffic to send. If they relayed to the White House every cable sent to the Pentagon, CIA, and State, the volume would swamp the Situation Room. Through a combination of shrewd manipulation and old-fashioned jawboning, Smith gradually began to get what he wanted flowing into the Situation Room.

Commander Shepard was nominally in charge of the Situation Room initially, and he assigned his assistant, Lieutenant Commander Gerry McCabe, to supervise the Situation Room upon its opening. The President had an aide from each service, each of whom supervised his own fiefdom in the White House. The naval aide, for example, managed, among other things, the White House Mess, Camp David, and the presidential yacht. The assignment of the Situation Room to one of his military aides was consistent with Kennedy's style.

De facto control of the Situation Room, however, devolved quickly to Bundy and Smith. (The White House Navy Administrative Unit provided funds for Situation Room activities through about 1963 when the NSC staff took complete responsibility for all facets of Situation Room operations.) They and Shepard agreed that CIA personnel should work in the Situation Room at night. Shepard said later that they immediately ruled out a staff of only military personnel because of the ongoing interservice rivalry at the White House. Colonel Godfrey

T. McHugh, Kennedy's Air Force aide, forwarded a Pentagon proposal to Kennedy on April 25, 1961, that called for the establishment of a "Nerve Center" for the White House, a facility that would be a "war room for the cold war." Smith later wrote that Kennedy turned down suggestions of a large facility and that the President asked Bundy to proceed with the smaller operation. Smith wrote that they selected the name *Situation Room* to make it clear that the facility was not a command center through which the President executed his commander-in-chief responsibilities.

CIA selected Charles D. "Chuck" Enright to be the first duty officer assigned to the Situation Room. He arrived in May 1961 and was scheduled to return to CIA in October 1962, but stayed on through November because of the Cuban Missile Crisis.

In an unpublished 1986 letter, Enright described his daily activities, which were far simpler then those of current duty officers:

> My workday, beginning at 9:30 AM, was 24 hours long, followed by 48 hours off. A typical day went as follows:
>
> 9:30 AM   Arrive at Sit Room, review night's activity.
>
> 10:00 AM   Go to NSC staff office, 3rd floor of Executive Office Building. Spend the next seven hours screening material for the NSC staff.
>
> 5:00 PM   Return to Sit Room, continue screening anything "hot."
>
> 5:30 PM   White House Staff Mess brings supper (for which I paid cash).
>
> 9:30 AM   (Next day) Duty ends.

At that time we did not produce summaries of events, just a log of our activities for the 24 hours. NSC staffers often stopped by in the morning to see if there was anything "hot" in their area of responsibility.

During Enright's tour in the Situation Room, his wife gave birth to their third child; her obstetrician was the same physician who attended Mrs. Kennedy when Caroline and John, Jr., were born. Enright recalled the event:

"During my wife's labor, Dr. Walsh asked her how to contact me and, to my distress, was given what he, of course, recognized as the White House number instead of our home phone number. My distress derived from my fear that he would thus equate my own financial means with that of my more affluent White House associates. I rectified this with him within a few days, assuring him that I had been working there, not visiting."

= = =

When the Situation Room opened for business in May 1961, the organization of President Kennedy's White House staff was still unsettled. Unlike the arrangements under subsequent presidents, Kennedy's national security adviser, McGeorge Bundy, controlled the flow of only a portion of the national security information into the Oval Office. This was because of the evolving nature of the national security adviser's role and the relationship of the National Security Council staff to the White House.

Congress created the National Security Council in 1947 during the Truman administration. A large staff sprang up around the NSC, complete with special committees for pushing prospective presidential decisions "up the policy hill" for NSC consideration and presidential approval, then down the hill for implementation and monitoring. Mostly professional bureaucrats or foreign service officers, the NSC staff was not considered part of the President's White House staff. In the 1950s, Eisenhower's national security advisers served as a bridge between the NSC staff and the White House.

Kennedy moved quickly to abolish much of the NSC support structure after his inauguration and consolidated the responsibilities of four or five people into McGeorge Bundy's portfolio. Bundy became Kennedy's personal adviser on national security matters. The remaining NSC staff became Bundy's staff and he organized them along some of the geographic and functional lines that still exist today. Bromley Smith, who had been the NSC executive secretary, kept the title but became Bundy's number three.

Despite Bundy's growing role in the spring of 1961, Kennedy's military assistant, Major General Ted Clifton, alone briefed Kennedy on intelligence developments. This practice was a hangover from Eisenhower's preference of Brigadier General Goodpaster as an intelligence briefer. In fact, Goodpaster remained at the White House temporarily to smooth the transfer to Clifton. Clifton debriefed Bundy after his sessions with the President and coordinated, with Bromley Smith and Bundy, the preparation of Kennedy's daily intelligence report. Clifton remained the primary intelligence liaison until Kennedy's assassination. Curiously, Bundy controlled the flow of intelligence reporting during crises, including Clifton in the distribution of crisis intelligence reporting to ensure coordination.

=== === ===

Throughout the rest of 1961, Bundy, his deputy Walt Rostow, and Bromley Smith consolidated the operations of the NSC staff and the Situation Room. The three had their offices adjacent to the Situation Room in the West Wing. In a January 1962 memo to Kennedy's assistant, Kenneth O'Donnell, Bundy strongly appealed for more space. "We are currently extremely crowded," Bundy wrote. "So is nearly everyone in the building, but our position is extreme. Come and see. (The President called it a pigpen, and my pride is hurt.)"

Bundy argued for a room to install teletype printers to allow the Situation Room to monitor newswire reports. He also asked for two more people, "a man and a girl" to help shuffle the national security paperwork for the President.

The Situation Room, upgraded as Bundy requested, established its role in crises during the Cuban Missile Crisis, a mission that continues to the present. On October 15, 1962, analysts at the National Photographic Interpretation Center (NPIC), examining aerial photographs taken the previous day by an U-2 reconnaissance aircraft, discovered Soviet offensive missiles in Cuba. In the ensuing days, the confrontation between the U.S. and the Soviet Union over those missiles almost precipitated nuclear war. Until November 1 when the Soviets began to dismantle the intermediate- and medium-range ballistic missiles in Cuba, the Situation Room duty officers performed the functions that Bundy had anticipated when he created the facility the year before. While the White House derived the most telling intelligence from the photos hand-carried to the White House daily from NPIC, the Situation Room screened incoming cables bearing on the crisis and passed them on to Bundy. White House staff members supplemented the duty officers at night by monitoring developments and answering presidential questions. Colonel L. J. Legere, an assistant to General Maxwell Taylor, Kennedy's military adviser, stood those watches and made the following entries in the Night Log on October 30–31:

> 9:00 *PM* *Called S/S Duty Officer to see what was going on over there. He will pass USUN 1550 electrically to the White House: it indicates U Thant made no progress today in Havana, hopes for better results tomorrow. Also earnestly requested no U.S. aerial reconnaissance tomorrow, 31 October. Stevenson and Sec'y Rusk discussed this information by phone.* [Note: S/S is Secretary of State; USUN 1550 is a cable from the U.S. mission at the United Nations; U Thant was the Secretary General of the UN

and went to Cuba to inspect the missile sites as part of the U.S.-Soviet agreement to end the crisis. Adlai Stevenson was U.S. Ambassador to the UN and Dean Rusk was Secretary of State.]

10:20 PM   Called Mr. Bromley Smith to report sense of USUN 1550. He said Sec'y Rusk had put out the gist of the message at the Exec Comm meeting at 1900 over at State. [Note: EXCOM was the Executive Committee of the National Security Council, the group of advisers that Kennedy met with throughout the crisis. It had met without the President at 7:00 P.M. earlier that day at the State Department.]

7:00 AM   Pulling together USUN 1547, USUN 1550 and Moscow 1145 for Smith-Bundy. Also Moscow 1146 and London 1724. The Moscow and London cables cover a Soviet request in Moscow for transit visa and overflight right for Mikoyan, who plans to leave Moscow November 1 and stop off 1 day in New York en route to Havana. [Note: These cables are identified by their origin—U.S. Embassy Moscow, U.S. Embassy London, etc.—and their serial number; Anastas I. Mikoyan was Soviet First Deputy Premier.]

President Kennedy met with the EXCOM in the Cabinet Room or Oval Office, rather than the smaller conference room in the Situation Room. There were meetings in the Situation Room during the crisis, but Bundy usually chaired them. One group, including Bobby Kennedy, Walt Rostow, and others, met on October 24 to review the status of the U.S. naval blockade of Cuba, the main thrust of the U.S. strategy to force the Soviets to remove the missiles. The duty officers kept a plot of the location of Soviet freighters en route to Cuba, as well as U.S. naval forces.

The "hotline" between Washington and Moscow didn't exist in the fall of 1962, so Kennedy and Nikita Khrushchev, the Soviet Secretary General, communicated via cables between embassies. As the crisis deepened, timely communiqués became crucial. Fearing that an U.S. invasion of Cuba was imminent and that normal diplomatic channels were too slow, Khrushchev released his capitulation response to Kennedy's ultimatum on Moscow's domestic news service. The Situation Room had an FBIS terminal (CIA's Foreign Broadcast Information Service monitored Soviet news broadcasts) and, according to Dino Brugioni's 1991 book *Eyeball to Eyeball*, the duty officers pulled Khrushchev's message off the FBIS teletype, paragraph by paragraph, and immediately sent them upstairs to the President.

=   =   =

By the spring of 1963, the Situation Room staff settled into an operational approach that remains, in broad terms, essentially unchanged through the present. The duty officers screened incoming cables and the wire service reports from Associated Press (AP), United Press International (UPI), and others. They distributed those reports to Bundy, Smith, NSC staff members, and, in the case of military messages, to the appropriate military aide to the President. They also posted and updated maps and charts (maps depict land, charts show ocean areas) and maintained a telephone watch with other government agencies. They kept the communications circuits in working order, including a special, dedicated line to London and a CIA circuit.

Art McCafferty, a CIA employee who started as a duty officer, but later transferred to the permanent NSC staff, became the de facto head of the Situation Room and reported to Smith and Bundy. But McCafferty was in an awkward position. The President's naval aide, Taz Shepard, still had nominal responsibility for the facility's operation and even assigned military personnel from his office to work in the Situation Room during the day. A CIA duty officer ran the Situation Room at night and on weekends and holidays. General Clifton, Kennedy's military assistant, still passed intelligence materials to the President, while, simultaneously, Bundy gave Kennedy everything else associated with national security. This split in supervision, staffing, and reporting was cumbersome, but collegial cooperation between Bundy, Shepard, and Clifton made it work to Kennedy's satisfaction. Walt Rostow said that McCafferty made sure the Situation Room performed its functions, despite the fractured nature of the organization. Upon Kennedy's assassination, Bundy, who became President Johnson's national security adviser, took complete control of the Situation Room.

3

ALERTING

The 2:00 A.M. Phone Call

"King Hussein's helicopter has crashed. . . . But he wasn't in it!"

As the director of the White House Situation Room, I tried to give the bottom line first when briefing senior officials. But as I walked up to John Poindexter, President Reagan's national security adviser, I realized I couldn't start off with the good news—"King Hussein is unhurt"—that might be confusing at best, ludicrous, actually. I had to mention the crash first. Predictably, Poindexter drew a sharp breath when he heard the word crash. He exhaled thankfully when I finished my sentence.

"Go tell George. He just went to the men's room."

As I waited outside the small West Wing bathroom—I had learned the difference between urgent and appropriate notification—I considered my approach to Secretary of State George Schultz. I stuck with the same line.

Secretary Schultz's eyes widened also, but he actually chuckled after I explained my bad news–good news predicament.

This nonevent from 1986 made news in the Reagan White

House because the Jordanian king was in the U.S. for a private visit. He had been traveling in a Sikorsky helicopter made available by the manufacturer as a courtesy to a good customer. When bad weather threatened flight safety that day, the King and his family opted to drive to their next stop. The aircraft crashed soon after the company pilots took off without their passengers. The crew died, regrettably, but the President and the country were spared the tragedy of the death of a foreign head of state on U.S. soil.

When President Kennedy created the Situation Room to keep better track of global events, he also wanted to be alerted to breaking events as soon as possible after they happened. The Situation Room succeeded because the duty officers did more than simply separate incoming information into piles of paper for the President and his staff to pick up for their morning reading. From the beginning, the staff has looked for something "hot" (to use the word of the first duty officer, Chuck Enright), which they passed immediately to the President's national security adviser. This alerting process is central to the mission of the Sit Room and the basis for all of its operations.

While the King Hussein alert was a little quirky, the incident was typical of many of the hundreds of alerts the Situation Room provide to the President and his staff over the course of a year. How the information reached John Poindexter and George Schultz is a good study of the alerting process in the Situation Room.

Helen Thomas, a long-time White House correspondent for the UPI newswire service, heard about the helicopter crash through her sources and asked White House Deputy Press Secretary Rusty Brashear what he knew about the accident. Unaware of the crash, Rusty asked me; I knew nothing, as well. I asked the duty officer to call the Federal Aviation Administration (FAA) and soon we had the details. During all this, President Reagan was meeting with his National Security Planning

Group (a gathering that included both Poindexter and Schultz) in the Sit Room conference room. Knowing that the incident did not merit interrupting the meeting, I nevertheless concluded that Poindexter should know about the crash in the event that the confusion about Hussein's presence aboard the aircraft persisted. I called Rusty with the details of the crash while I waited for the meeting to end. Rusty closed the loop with Thomas, who in turn filed her story on the UPI wire. When the meeting broke up, I walked with Poindexter up the stairs to his office and briefed him, however awkwardly, on the event.

The Situation Room uses a series of increasingly restrictive criteria for judging the relative significance of incoming information. Although computer algorithms help identify information associated with known situations, the responsibility of judging whether someone up the line should be alerted about an event falls almost completely on the duty officer. Through excellent training, experience, and collegial coordination with other watch centers, the duty officers almost always get it right.

The increasingly finer sieves through which the duty officers sift data help discard irrelevant information, identify events that should be included in the Sit Room's twice-daily summaries, or select events that someone should know about soonest. The last category encompasses two levels of immediacy. If King Hussein had been in the helicopter when it crashed, I would have interrupted Reagan's meeting and slipped a note to Poindexter. Even with the king unhurt, the incident was too important to wait for the evening summary, so I briefed Poindexter and Schulz after the meeting.

Although the Situation Room duty officers shoulder enormous responsibility, others help them watch for Armageddon. National security-related information flows into the White House through several portals. First, the President's Cabinet members call him routinely to pass along important nuggets, a

process that can easily approach a serious game of one-upman-
ship. Those principal advisers also call the President's national
security adviser to relay news about an event. Subcabinet officials, such as an assistant secretary of state, call members of
the NSC staff to exchange information. The news media,
whether it's Helen Thomas passing a tidbit to the Press Office
or CNN broadcasting news about a bombing of a U.S. embassy, insert information directly into the White House. But
the Situation Room processes the vast majority of information
that enters the White House, that data generated by the "system," the national security communications apparatus of the
U.S. government and its closest allies. But because of the time
differences between Washington and potential trouble spots
around the globe—Afghanistan, the Balkans, Middle East,
Far East, and Pacific—many untoward events that merit alerting happen at night, eastern standard time (EST). Since the
Situation Room works 24/7, the likelihood of the duty officers
catching something first increases after working hours in
Washington.

Why must the Situation Room alert people about major international and domestic events? Setting aside for the moment
a surprise nuclear missile attack from Russia or a "rogue" nation, the need for alerting boils down to three issues. One,
what does the event mean to the national security of the
United States? Two, what should the U.S. government do
about the event? And three, how should the White House respond to news media questions about what the U.S. government is doing about the event. The speed at which all this
happens—event, alerting, consideration, and public announce-
ment—has been increasing at a maddening rate since the establishment of the Situation Room. Alexander Haig, who
worked his way up from Henry Kissinger's military assistant to
White House chief of staff during Nixon's presidency (and
from Army lieutenant colonel to four-star general along the

way), described the urgency of the process. "In the old order, presidents had time to wait for federal agencies to analyze a crisis and make recommendations. The President could make decisions calmly and after due deliberation. But technology has compressed the time between an event itself and the time at which the President has to deal with the event."

The Situation Room performs its alerting functions as long as the "system" sends meaningful information to the White House. With considerable and critical active support from President Kennedy in 1961, Bromley Smith, the executive secretary of the NSC, began the continuing process of getting sources of national security information to send data to the White House. Important sources, both then and now, are U.S. embassies abroad. Ambassadors frequently send descriptions and analyses of events occurring in their host countries. At first, Smith had to ask the State Department to relay those cabled reports to the Situation Room. Later, as embassy–State–White House communications cooperation matured, certain embassy reports were routed directly to the White House.

Another hugely important source of information has been the U.S. foreign intelligence community. Although key allies—Great Britain, Canada, Australia, and New Zealand—also contribute useful information through exchange agreements, the alphabet soup of U.S. intelligence agencies generate most of the classified data. CIA, DIA, NSA, NIMA (National Imagery and Mapping Agency), and the military intelligence services produce thousands of electronically transmitted messages every day. Other federal agencies that have intelligence operations—FBI; DEA (Drug Enforcement Administration); FEMA (Federal Emergency Management Agency); the Departments of Justice, Energy, and Transportation; and the Coast Guard—also generate intelligence messages.

CIA generally produces most of the government's human intelligence, that which is generated by either CIA operations officers or foreign agents they recruit. CIA also has the mandate to generate finished intelligence products on national issues such as arms control and terrorism. NSA, assisted by the military service cryptologic and security agencies, produces signals intelligence, information derived from intercepted foreign communications, electronic, and radar systems. DIA produces military intelligence and coordinates the intelligence collection and reporting of U.S. military attaches assigned to U.S. embassies overseas. The services, despite what appears to be, a priori, an overlap with DIA, report on foreign military activities relevant to their respective service.

The Defense Department (DoD) also generates electronic messages (State calls them cables; in the Pentagon, it's a message) that the White House needs. Reports of serious accidents, progress reports during wars and military interventions, and force disposition summaries are examples of important military messages that the Situation Room has always requested.

If all three major producers of cables (messages to you, General) had sent every message to the new Situation Room, both Bromley Smith and the communications circuits would have been overwhelmed. Luckily, that did not happen, mainly because these agencies didn't want the President to see everything, and certainly nothing before the heads of those agencies saw it first. So Smith and Art McCafferty, the first Sit Room director, as well as every director since had to negotiate for the right cables. Smith devised a means for the agencies to pare down the traffic, which, in broad terms, continues today. Throughout most of the government, organizations that originate cables assign each one a precedence codeword that indicates its relative importance and perishability—"Routine," "Priority," "Immediate," and "Flash" in ascending order. Smith asked the agencies to relay all cables with a precedence of Priority or higher to the White House. While this tactic helped refine the traffic load, ambassadors around the world soon learned of this automatic screening process and attempted to get the White House to notice their otherwise routine reporting by stamping "Priority" on virtually every cable.

Over the years, Situation Room directors have met with the heads of the watch centers at each agency that produces information the Sit Room needed. When I say "needed," I really mean "required in order to answer questions from the President or his national security adviser." Art McCafferty worked diligently to make the process work, and his successor, David McManis, sought to refine the system. "I spent a lot of time trying to place the responsibility for selection of information on the agencies and departments so that the White House got the cream off the top of the milk bottle," McManis said.

Other directors have sought to install procedures that helped the producing agencies identify issues that should be forwarded to the Situation Room. I started the Weekly Emphasis List that continues today: each week, the Sit Room staff compiled a list of trouble spots and issues that the NSC staff was watching carefully and faxed it to the other watch centers. It also helped the Situation Room duty officers who were coming in off a break or vacation to get back up to speed.

The Sit Room started the daily NATSEC in the 1990s, a secure conversation between the Washington area watch centers—the NATional SECurity conference call. It is essentially a daily version of the Emphasis List.

The most important alerting coordination system during crises has been the NOIWON—the National Operations and Intelligence Watch Office Network. Art McCafferty started the Washington Area Operations and Command Center Committee (WAOCCC), not only to help coordinate reporting, but also to seek efficient alerting procedures for crises. The WAOCCC sponsors the operation of the NOIWON. When the first report of a potentially serious situation is distributed, one of the member agencies, usually the one that generated that first report, initiates a NOIWON call. The conference call permits the watch centers to exchange information, compare notes, and discuss additional sources that might be used to collect information on the event.

Sally Botsai, first an analyst, then deputy director in the Situation Room during the mid-1970s, remembers the NOIWON. "It seemed that most time-sensitive or fast-breaking developments took place in the early hours of the morning, while the principals at each agency were sleeping," said Botsai. "The custom, after the substantive portion of the NOIWON call ended, was to ask who was going to wake up whom among the movers and shakers. We needed to know if the Pentagon or State intended to wake up their Secretary. If so, we had to call the national security adviser because he would be an angry principal had one of his counterparts gotten the news before him, and vice versa. So NOIWON calls were for both exchanging intelligence and coordinating wake-up calls."

A huge disparity has existed among presidents regarding the amount of detail each wanted and about which they wanted to be notified immediately. The all-time champ was Lyndon Johnson. In the 1950s, as a result of Eisenhower's dissatisfaction with the time that it took to get an emergency message to the White House, NSA created the CRITICOM communications system. NSA designed the system to get an alert message to the White House from an intelligence producer in ten minutes or less. The alert messages were called CRITICs and Johnson decreed that he wanted to be called on every CRITIC, despite the fact that there were often hundreds a month.

In those days, there was a fair number of CRITICs that simply did not merit immediate presidential notification, so Art McCafferty had to decide whether he should call the President. "When Art did hold back on a CRITIC," recalls McManis, who worked for McCafferty before later becoming director, "and LBJ later heard about it, Rostow really beat up Art. But Art was always right, LBJ didn't need to be bothered with all those calls." Of course, there have been plenty of legitimate CRITICs, so McCafferty was under pressure to make the right call. Luckily, most other presidents have preferred that all such calls be routed through their national security adviser, giving the Situation Room director the chance to discuss the significance of the CRITIC with a senior staff member.

"Johnson wanted to be the first to know about an incident," said Walt Rostow, Johnson's national security adviser. "When someone briefed him on an event, Johnson listened intently and never let on that he already knew the details."

Every duty officer throughout the history of the Situation Room has yearned for the opportunity to personally brief the President. Whether it was a trip to the Oval Office, known as "rug time"—standing on the big carpet in the Oval Office—or just a phone call, taking the news to the President was the absolute highlight of the assignment. Over the years, the alerting process provided most of the opportunities for a one-on-one with the chief executive.

Dave Radi, a duty officer under Reagan and Bush recalled one of his moments with President Bush. "A Soviet attack submarine, a one-of-a-kind, titanium-hulled MIKE class, sank in 1989," said Radi. "While every agency reported on the disaster, I got the best info from the Office of Naval Intelligence." Radi, a naval intelligence officer who had served in the Navy's Washington intelligence center, Intelligence Plot, before going to the Situation Room, took advantage of his connections with the Office of Naval Intelligence (ONI).

"I called ONI to make sure I had all available intelligence," said Radi. "Brent Scowcroft, Bush's national security adviser, was on vacation in Utah, so I briefed Bob Gates, his deputy, on everything we had. To my surprise, Gates took me down the hall to the Oval to brief the President and, despite my nervousness, I did pretty well. I answered all of President Bush's questions except the one I was not prepared for—'Are we in any position to render assistance to the submarine?' In retrospect, I should have anticipated such a question from him in view of his rescue after his plane was shot down in World War II."

Yet however exciting a trip to the Oval Office might be, it could also be hard on the nerves. Most duty officers had the important information down pat, but feared tripping on the edge of the rug or dropping something. Kevin O'Connell, an analyst in the Situation Room during the early 1990s, recalled the widely repeated story of Steve Baker, a Marine duty officer who took an important CRITIC up to the President. "Steve opened the door and found that President Bush, with Brent Scowcroft at his side, was in the middle of a phone call," O'Connell said. "I guess Steve was distracted by the bad timing of his entrance and failed to notice that Millie, Bush's dog, was asleep on the floor and accidentally stepped on her tail. Steve went one way, Millie another, and the President gave Steve a stern look."

George H. W. Bush and Johnson were the presidents who wanted the most detail and engaged in a running dialogue with the Sit Room duty officers. While some presidents were simply aloof and almost never spoke with the Situation Room staff— Nixon and Reagan are the best examples—the minimal direct communications between the Sit Room and most presidents are more a function of the greater role of the national security adviser after Kennedy and Johnson. The national security adviser, or his (or her, in the case of Condoleezza Rice) deputy, funneled information from the Situation Room to the President, and they wanted one voice speaking to the President.

Under George H. W. Bush, Brent Scowcroft set up an NSC structure that encouraged the free flow of information, both up to the President and down to the Situation Room, according to Kevin O'Connell. "General Scowcroft and his deputy, Bob Gates, believed that the person with the most knowledge about a situation should be the one talking to the President," O'Connell said. "Plus, President Bush was an extremely knowledgeable customer, having been the DCI, Vice President, and envoy to China. For an intelligence officer, it was a pleasure to brief him because he understood everything."

Bob O'Hara, an analyst from NSA who worked for both Reagan and Bush, echoes O'Connell's feelings about George H. W. Bush. "President Bush was knowledgeable about world events. I called him in the middle of the night to tell him about a hijacking in the Middle East, said O'Hara. "After I covered everything we had about the hijacking, he started grilling me about events in Nicaragua and Panama! I was sure glad that I was up to speed on everything that morning. He was an intelligence officer's dream."

Process

Most often, the duty officer first calls the director of the Situation Room, seeking either confirmation that he has caught something meaningful, or advice on whom else to contact. Beyond the director, most of the alerting phone calls that Situation Room duty officers make are to either the national security adviser or a member of the NSC staff. The NSC staff member is more often able to synthesize the reported event with other known information, thus assigning more, or even less, importance to the report. The NSC staff is divided into geographical and functional offices; every situation that arises in the world will fall into at least one staff member's portfolio.

Important developments always land in the lap of the national security adviser or his or her deputy. They make the decision about presidential notification, and their decisions are not only based on the significance of the event, but also on their relationship with the President and on the President's style. They also determine whom outside the NSC sphere should receive alerting information, especially people like the President's chief of staff and domestic advisers who might not know how to evaluate unrefined information. Bob Gates said there were grave risks associated with people who were inexperienced in the subtleties of intelligence reporting getting a hold of a report out of context. "I saw it happen several times," said Gates. "Someone got access to a raw report, set their hair on fire, and ran down to the Oval Office. The national security adviser then had to put Humpty Dumpty back together again."

In some instances, the duty officers are thrown a curve ball and don't know whom to contact. "The Sit Room paged me while I was attending a New Year's Eve party," said Jim Steinberg, deputy national security adviser to Clinton. "The duty officer said, 'The Coast Guard has picked up El Duque, what shall we do?'" On December 31, 1997, legendary Cuban baseball pitcher Orlando "El Duque" Hernandez, left Cuba with several others on a boat bound for Florida, but became marooned on a small island where the Coast Guard found them. It was U.S. policy then to return any Cuban who had not reached the U.S. So when the U.S. allowed El Duque and two others into the country several days later, but sent the rest of the group back to Cuba, there was a bit of a political, diplomatic, and legal brouhaha. Hernandez, whose brother played for the Florida Marlins, ultimately signed with the New York Yankees.

"After I told the duty officer who to notify," said Steinberg, "I began to speculate, along with others at the party, which team would sign El Duque."

Carl Kaysen, deputy national security adviser to Kennedy, also recalled a story about Cuban refugees that occurred in the early 1960s.

"The duty officer called one night to report that a Cuban ship was off Miami and it was displaying a large sign that read

'CIA HELP.' As we later learned, the crew had mutinied, tied up the captain, and sailed to Miami. The duty officer connected me to the Navy admiral who headed the Eastern Sea Frontier. I told him to let anyone come ashore who so desired, untie the captain, and let him and any others who wanted to return, go back to Cuba. I also told him, 'No press.'"

Nuclear War

There is one alerting process in which the Situation Room rarely participates—"The Big War." While the U.S. could conceivably start an unprovoked nuclear war, most cold war scenarios had the U.S. retaliating in response to a preemptive strike from the Soviets. Thus, a considerable portion of the national defense establishment, albeit one that has never been used in full (thankfully), is designed to detect a missile attack on the U.S. The system then alerts the President and his most senior national security advisers—the people whom the military refer to as the National Command Authority—within minutes of the missiles' launch. If the commander-in-chief of the North American Aerospace Defense Command believes that missile attack is real, he confers with the National Military Command Center (NMCC) in the Pentagon. If they concur, NMCC will initiate a conference call to include, at the least, the chairman of the Joint Chiefs of Staff, the Secretary of Defense, the national security adviser, and the President. The call to the President would go through WHCA's telephone switchboard, known as "Signal," rather than the Situation Room. The conferees must decide how to respond to the attack.

All of this must be done quickly, because U.S. strategy has called for "launch on warning"—firing our own nuclear weapons before they can be destroyed by the incoming enemy attack—thus guaranteeing "mutual assured destruction" of both parties to the war. Because of the potential threat of an enemy strike without a prior run-up of nonnuclear hostilities, a "bolt from the blue" attack is the worst-case scenario and the White House must prepare accordingly. The White House Military Office is the primary link between the President and the Big War participants—the early warning systems, the ballistic missile submarines at sea, the strategic bombers in the air, and the ICBMs in silos out on the Dakota prairies. They are there to help the President execute his duties as Commander in Chief of the Armed Forces during a surprise nuclear attack.

Most recently run by a civilian, the Military Office is the emergency planning and operations branch of the White House staff. Within the office, there are five military aides to the President, one from each service and the Coast Guard, and they rotate the responsibility of staying near the President. They carry the "football," a briefcase that contains reference documents that outline U.S. strategic attack options, communications instructions, and the codewords that the President would use to authorize the release of nuclear weapons in response to an enemy attack. If there were an actual attack, the aide, often seen on the periphery of TV coverage of the President, would be notified at the same time as the President of a missile launch. The aide would rush to the President's side with the football and help the President go through predetermined response alternatives.

The Military Office is also responsible for getting the President out of Washington, spiriting him off to predesignated locations where he can safely run the government if the nation is under attack. Early on, the bomb shelter in the East Wing basement was a safe refuge, but bigger and bigger Soviet nuclear weapons made that site unfit except for conventional attacks on the White House. The shelter is called the President's Emergency Operations Center (PEOC) and inside its blast doors were workstations, bunks, emergency rations, and water. When terrorists crashed airliners into the World Trade Center towers and the Pentagon in September 2001 and President

Bush was traveling, the Secret Service escorted Vice President Cheney to the PEOC when they thought a plane was headed for the White House.

Incidentally, the PEOC has always reserved a seat for a representative from the Sit Room in the event of an attack on the White House. I always wondered, as have many in the Sit Room, how we would have chosen that person. Luckily, that decision never had to be made.

The U.S. and its allies have spent huge sums of money over the years preparing for this worst case—a surprise attack, in which we had to "use or lose" our weapons in response to an enemy attack. Moreover, there was always the possibility of an accidental launch of a nuclear-armed missile. We had to acknowledge these Armageddon scenarios because there was a chance, however slight, that they might happen. More probably a nuclear exchange might have occurred as an escalation of a conventional war or some other precursor hostilities. We came close to nuclear war with the Soviets during the Cuban Missile Crisis, but that possibility arose only after a period of confrontation and increasing tensions. The threatened Soviet intervention in the 1967 Arab-Israeli Six-Day War or a possible conventional conflict between NATO and the Warsaw Pact in Europe could have been the beginnings of a nuclear war. However, many intelligence professionals never believed that the Soviets were ever capable of initiating a bolt-from-the-blue strategic attack on the U.S. without generating their forces to full-alert status beforehand, a process generally observable to the West.

So, at least from my perspective from the Situation Room in the mid-1980s, the time when Reagan was pushing the Soviets into an arms buildup that eventually bankrupted the U.S.S.R., I never considered a bolt-from-the-blue attack to be one of my daily problems. We never participated in missile warning exercises or simulated attacks or practiced ducking under our desks. We never saw the football, much less got a peek inside.

However, Bill Odom, military assistant to President Carter's National Security Adviser Zbigniew Brzezinski, did organize a drill that involved the Situation Room and President Carter. "We convinced the President to participate in a nuclear release drill," said Odom. "The Situation Room connected all the parties on a secure phone with the President. The CINCs (commanders-in-chief of the various military units involved in the exercise) all tried to sound authoritative and some even lowered their voices to emphasize their seriousness. But I could tell that most of them were nervous being on the phone with the President."

The generals had plenty to be nervous about because Odom said Carter found the notebook that contained U.S. attack options hard to follow. "Carter told them to redesign the instructions and come back and try it again," said Odom more than twenty years later. "The new layout was a huge step forward in user friendliness."

America has never had to confront actual nuclear attacks, but there have been some scary moments. Robert Gates, a former DCI, wrote in his memoir about one false alarm—a Soviet missile attack during Carter's term. Gates wrote that Brzezinski got a call one night that warning systems had detected 2,200 Soviet missiles en route to the U.S. About to call Carter, Brzezinski discovered that someone had inserted a military exercise tape in a computer.

The Western news media reported in 1998 that Russia suffered a similar false alarm in 1995 when Norway launched a research rocket designed to examine the Northern Lights. The missile triggered a Russian alert that led to Russian President Boris Yeltsin opening up his own "football" before the confusion ended.

The irony of the Situation Room's role in the Big War was evident in a 1977 story in the *New York Times* with the title, "On Watch in the White House Basement for Armageddon."

In the article, Dennis Chapman, then the director of the Situation Room, described its function and operations, but it was the title that grabbed the attention of a special type of reader.

"We started getting letters and phone calls from all the weirdos who were on the lookout for the anti-Christ," explained Chapman. "They were pleased that we, too, were on watch and they were glad the administration was on their side!"

Domestic Situations

"It's the Economy, Stupid!"

This, of course, was the famous slogan that Bill Clinton's campaign staff kept taped to the wall in its war room. When Clinton took office on January 20, 1993, he and his staff brought that emphasis on domestic issues to a White House Situation Room that historically had been focused on international affairs. There were news reports that the President's staff considered the establishment of a domestic situation room in the White House or the nearby Old Executive Office Building where representatives from domestic agencies could coordinate their actions.

While that didn't happen, President Clinton established the National Economic Council (NEC) in January 1993. This body was to follow the model of the National Security Council, coordinating economic policy just as the NSC coordinated foreign policy. The two councils had overlapping staffs and the NEC even met in the Situation Room. Clinton also added Robert Rubin, the first head of the NEC, to the National Security Council. In 2001, President Bush established the Homeland Security Council, also using the NSC as a model.

Neil O'Leary recalled the primary interest of the incoming Clinton administration. "The new President and his staff were clearly focused on domestic policy issues at the start of the administration," O'Leary said. "Their interest was such that I had to organize a domestic alerting system where there was none before. We were not prepared for the fire at the Branch Davidian complex in Waco, Texas, for example, and I realized that I couldn't rely on just the news media to report earthquakes and fires."

O'Leary approached Phil Lader for help. He had been the organizer of the "Renaissance Weekends" that the Clintons attended annually in Hilton Head and came to the White House as deputy chief of staff. "I enlisted his help in contacting agencies like the Federal Emergency Management Agency and the Department of Interior to ask them to forward information about untoward incidents in the U.S.—an emergency reporting system to parallel that which funneled reporting on international events to the Situation Room. By the time I left in August 1993, I had an around-the-clock point of contact for every agency in the executive branch."

Tony Lake, President Clinton's first national security adviser, recalled another domestic incident early in Clinton's first term that tested the presumed distinctions between domestic and international crisis reporting.

"In 1993 the terrorist bombing of the World Trade Center in New York caught us off-guard," said Lake. "Someone on the domestic side tried to manage the incident initially, but I volunteered the NSC staff in order to bring more order to the process." Lake and his staff soon realized there was only one Situation Room at the White House and that the facility had to pay attention to everything, domestic and international.

O'Leary did not know it in 1993, but earlier Sit Room personnel struggled with the same issue of domestic crises. Chuck Enright, the first duty officer in the Situation Room, recalled in a 1986 letter how they had become involved in the federal integration of the University of Mississippi. "Attorney General Bobby Kennedy arranged for a direct phone line from the U.S. Army command post on the campus back to the Situation

Room," wrote Enright. "The Army called us twice a day, but we never had anything to tell them."

In 1966, Art McCafferty, director of the Situation Room for much of the 1960s, wrote to Leo Bourassa, director of the White House's Office of Emergency Planning, asking that Bourassa's Alert Center notify the Situation Room of the following events:

- Natural catastrophes—Major earthquakes, tornadoes, hurricanes, and floods, especially those that required the use of military forces for assistance;
- Major power failures or communications blackouts; and
- Accidents involving nuclear materials or toxic chemicals.

Joe Shergalis, a duty officer under President Johnson, recalled a tragic domestic incident that caught the attention of the First Family. "A sniper barricaded himself at the top of the tower at the University of Texas, shooting people on the ground below," said Shergalis. "Luci Johnson came down to the Sit Room and stood next to me as I watched the incoming wire service reports about the shooting. She had been a student at Texas and wanted to see if she knew any of the victims."

During the Nixon administration, his domestic advisers also wanted to build a domestic situation room, according to David McManis, director of the Situation Room at that time. "They were concerned with the antiwar demonstrations and wanted a place where a staff could monitor the events," recalled McManis. "They wanted to construct a facility but couldn't, so they moved into the old bomb shelter in the East Wing basement. They installed TV monitors to watch video feeds from around town. It didn't last long."

Just as Art McCafferty had done, McManis also reached out to domestic agencies, asking for any information of domestic disasters. "Art had organized the Washington WAOCCC to help coordinate the sharing of crisis information between operations centers," said McManis. "We used that organization to compile a list of government agencies that might be involved in domestic situations and gather twenty-four-hour-a-day contacts and phone numbers." Had Neil O'Leary, who did the same thing in 1993, known what planning had preceded him, he might have quoted Yogi Berra: "It was déjà vu all over again."

I had a brief question in my mind in 1986 when the U.S. space shuttle *Challenger* exploded just after lift-off.

Although shuttle launches had become lesser news media events, CNN still covered every lift-off. After watching the pieces of the shuttle fall to the sea, I asked myself, "Is this my deal?" After all, it *was* a domestic incident. But considering the magnitude of the tragedy, it had to be my deal. I ran upstairs and broke the most sacred protocol in the White House—I opened office doors without an appointment. I first told John Poindexter, Reagan's national security adviser, then Vice President Bush, then the President's chief of staff, Donald Regan: "The shuttle exploded just after launch. Turn on your TV." After leaving Regan's office, I joined a river of people moving toward the Oval Office, where we met the President's secretary, Cathy Osbourne, who opened the door. Soon a dozen people stood in the Oval Office with President Reagan watching CNN replay the explosion over and over again.

Everyone wanted more information. We had to act, regardless of whether it was an international or domestic situation. Back in the Situation Room, I called the head of NASA and invited him to use my office as his command center. He arrived within thirty minutes. We set up two phone lines on speakers in the conference room and contacted both the Johnson Space Center in Houston and the Kennedy Space Center in Florida. They passed us information as they received it; we smoothed it out and sent reports upstairs. After it was clear there were no survivors, we disbanded the operation.

When terrorists crashed airliners into the World Trade Towers and the Pentagon in 2001, the Situation Room staff also instantly determined that they had to act immediately. Some things simply transcend the boundary between domestic and international events.

There was a particular situation during the Kennedy administration that was indeed a domestic problem, but one with a little different meaning—John Kennedy's relations with his wife. Seymour Hersh's 1997 book, *The Dark Side of Camelot*, a volume not well received by the Kennedy family, reported that Mrs. Kennedy wired the Situation Room in advance of her return when she traveled without the President. Hersh wrote that Lieutenant Commander Gerry McCabe, the assistant naval aide to President Kennedy and the daytime supervisor of the Situation Room, told him in 1995 of the impact of a change in the First Lady's travel plans. If she wired that she was coming home early, it meant that the President's paramours should leave the White House before she returned. Rear Admiral McCabe's widow, Joy Dell, confirmed that President Kennedy's military aides, her husband included, were aware of the President's extramarital affairs and that Hersh's account was accurate.

Impact of the News Media

"Mike, it's Karen. Are you awake? A Pan Am plane has been hijacked in Karachi." Thus came a report from the duty officer in an early morning call. "The hijacker took control of the plane while it was still on the ground, but we have no information about what's going on inside the aircraft. The Pakistanis have the plane surrounded and they are attempting to talk with the guy with the guns. The only source we have is CNN."

I received a lot of phone calls like this one, mostly at night, during the mid-1980s. Terrorism and hostage taking dominated my days and nights during the second Reagan administration. In instances like the Pan Am hijacking, quite a few White House staff members wanted the facts and wanted them immediately. We tapped every source of information to meet that demand—satellites, clandestine agents, overseas embassies, military intelligence, and the news media. But since the mid-1980s, the medium that has gained almost preeminent standing among the traditional sources of information is cable TV news networks.

After the duty officer's call, I dressed and arrived at the Situation Room at 6:00 A.M. CNN was still the only source of information on the hijacking. The State Department Operations Center called soon to report that embassy personnel in Islamabad could not reach Karachi for several hours. CIA, the National Security Agency, and the Pentagon had nothing to add.

I briefed John Poindexter, Don Regan, Vice President Bush's assistant, and several NSC staff members. Returning to the Situation Room, I found the watch officers in a dither. CNN was off the air.

In 1986, Washington, D.C., was not wired for cable TV. The White House received CNN and other cable channels from George Mason University in Fairfax, Virginia. The university picked up CNN on their satellite dish and sent the signal to us as part of their daily programming. At least that was the pattern during most of the day. CNN was not widely watched then, so George Mason often substituted other shows on early weekday mornings. On that morning, they were broadcasting a home study course—Economics 101.

CNN's Washington office could not help me, so I called George Mason's TV studio. A drowsy student, probably there all night, was surprised to hear my request.

"I am the director of the White House Situation Room," I

said in my most authoritative voice. "An airliner has been hijacked in Pakistan and CNN is our most productive source of information. Can you put the CNN feed back on the line to the White House?"

"The White House?" he gasped. "Wow! Sure, whatever you want, I guess. What if my boss gets mad? Will you talk to him?"

Within minutes of assuring him of a follow-up phone call, I turned to see the familiar talking head reappear on the TV.

Cable news television networks have profoundly influenced the operations of not only the Situation Room, but also the White House as a whole. First, CNN has become a valuable source of breaking information in all watch centers, not just the Situation Room. Second, it has decreased the reaction time that the President has after an event to formulate and disseminate the U.S. position on the event. Third, world leaders can conduct international diplomacy via CNN, quickly sending a message around the world instead of using the slower communications through embassies. Last, CNN brings real-time images to the public, either helping to support a government action or quickly undermining an ill-conceived initiative.

The Alerting Process

"My most important source of information on breaking events when I ran the Situation Room was the news media, especially CNN," said Kevin Cosgriff, who was assigned there from 1997 to 1999. "Their news-gathering operation is so widespread and so nimble that no government collection system could match it." (While CNN was the "firstest with the mostest," other cable news operators such as MSNBC and Fox News are also useful sources to the Sit Room.)

Since the mid-1980s, every watch center, not only in Washington, but also around the world, has tuned in CNN. In between crises, Sit Room duty officers have fallen in love with the weather girl, wearily watched the exercise segments from "Body by Jake," and suffered through the advertisements for Zamfir and his pan flute. Yet they kept their TV tuned to CNN so that they could catch the first hint of a new international or domestic situation. They screened CNN like they screened cables. One watch center even initiated a NOIWON crisis conference call based on a CNN report, momentarily forgetting that everyone else was also watching the same television show. The CNN revolution was not unlike the revolution that President Kennedy led by installing the communications circuits in the West Wing basement in 1961. Each vastly increased the speed at which information entered the White House.

Robert Gates, who held a variety of posts at the CIA and the NSC staff from the 1970s to the 1990s, was deputy national security adviser to President George H. W. Bush before Gates' appointment as director of Central Intelligence. At his DCI confirmation hearings, Gates told senators that he thought the cable news channels were scooping the intelligence community. Tony Lake, Clinton's first national security adviser, said that while CNN was very useful, it could mislead viewers. "The TV camera often takes one image and turns it into a general picture in the viewer's eye," said Lake. "In order not to lose the context of that single image, I would have liked to have seen our embassy dispatch a political officer to the event, just as CNN sends a crew, to become a second eyewitness. That officer could then file a timely report that could add perspective to the TV image."

But presidents watch CNN, as well as duty officers. "President Bush kept CNN on in his study," recalled Dave Radi, a duty officer during the early 1990s. "When he saw something interesting, he called us and asked if we had any additional information."

Decreased Reaction Time

CNN is indeed a powerful weapon for the Situation Room to use in the war on slow reporting, but it can be a two-edged sword. While some events may be known to the President through only intelligence sources, thus giving the White House a head start over the news media, most reporting on international events today is available simultaneously to every one with a television. In many cases, presidential notification is followed shortly by the news media asking his press secretary what the President thinks about the event. A bombing in Kenya? What is the President doing about it? The White House is now operating at "CNN speed," which means the Press Office must react more rapidly to news media questions. As a result, one of the Situation Room's primary customers for heads-up phone calls is the President's deputy press secretary for NSC matters.

Roman Popadiuk, seconded to the Situation Room from State as one of my duty officers in 1985, became an assistant to Ed Djerejian, the NSC spokesman under Reagan. President Bush later promoted Popadiuk to the NSC position under Press Secretary Marlin Fitzwater. Roman put in a long day in that job, leaving his home at 6:30 A.M. and listening to his car radio for new developments around the world. Arriving at his office, Roman scanned the front pages of the *Washington Post* and *New York Times* and glanced at the White House News Summary, a compendium of top news stories prepared by staff in the Press Office. At about 7:10 A.M., Roman talked with the Sit Room duty officer and sifted through the cables and reports that the duty officers had placed in his box. He then met briefly with Brent Scowcroft, Bush's national security adviser, or Scowcroft's deputy, Robert Gates, to coordinate the NSC's position on the day's news events. At 8:30 A.M., Roman joined the rest of the Press Office in a meeting with Fitzwater to prepare for the daily White House press briefing. Then, Roman checked in with the Sit Room before the noon briefing to see if there were any updates on ongoing events. At the daily briefing, Roman answered reporters' questions about national security matters. If nothing else happened that day, Roman dropped in the Situation Room before heading for home at 7:30 P.M.

"In the foreign policy area, the Situation Room was a valuable asset to the Press Office," said Popadiuk. "They provided me with not only updates on developing events, but also intelligence on matters that may be coming into the public domain. The latter was especially important because the intelligence kept the Press Office from being blindsided or misspeaking about an event."

P. J. Crowley was the deputy press secretary for the NSC during the last three years of the Clinton administration and remembered its challenges. "As the spokesman for the President on national security issues, I was only as good as the information I was given," said Crowley. "I had to stay ahead of the news media, and I could only do that with help from the Situation Room. More often than not, the Sit Room briefed me on an event before most of the media knew about it so I could respond to media questions quickly and accurately. But if a reporter asked me about something for which I was unprepared, my first call was to the Situation Room. The Sit Room is the lifeblood of the National Security Council, and its oxygen."

On-Air International Diplomacy

Presidents G. H. W. Bush and Reagan and their advisers used cable news services to quickly send messages abroad. Johanna

Neuman, formerly the foreign editor for *USA Today*, wrote in her 1996 book, *Lights, Camera, War*, about how Bush's Secretary of State James Baker sent a message to Iraq's Saddam Hussein just days before the start of the Gulf War in 1991. Speaking in front of U.S. warplanes in Taif, Saudi Arabia, Baker reiterated the demand from the U.S.-led coalition that Iraq pull out of Kuwait before the January 15 deadline. His speech was covered by CNN, and Neuman quoted Baker as saying, "We didn't send that message through Joe Wilson (top U.S. diplomat in Baghdad). We sent it through CNN."

Sol Levine, a former executive producer at CNN for White House coverage, recalled an instance late in the Reagan second term when CNN was covering the issue of U.S. recognition of the Palestinian Liberation Organization (PLO). They were briefed on the White House position, along with other news media representatives, then a CNN reporter delivered a live stand-up report from the North Lawn of the White House. Levine said that Colin Powell, then Reagan's national security adviser, whose office overlooked the North Lawn, pulled aside the curtains in his window and gave the CNN crew a thumbs-up. "I assume he was telling us that we not only got the story right, but also had delivered the White House's message," said Levine.

Real-time Images to the Public

While CNN has enabled world leaders to leapfrog traditional diplomatic procedures, it has also brought almost instantaneous feedback to those leaders from the public at large. Certainly the public watched newsreels and examined photos of the fighting in World War II and Korea, but filmmakers and photographers were carefully kept from the gruesome sights of American dead and wounded. TV coverage of the war in Vietnam brought frightening images of death to the public, especially during the North Vietnamese Tet Offensive, and public support for the war eroded. But now, unedited, live TV coverage of world events has an even greater impact, not only on the public, but also on government decision makers. The 1989 image of a lone demonstrator in front of Chinese tanks in Beijing's Tiananmen Square is one example. Coverage of Boris Yeltsin atop a Russian tank in Moscow during the attempted coup against Mikhail Gorbachev in 1991 galvanized viewers. Images of Kurdish refugees fleeing Iraq in 1991 are reported to be the basis for a change in the Bush administration's position on aid to the Kurds. A video of Somalis dragging the dead body of an American through the streets of Mogadishu in 1993 immediately generated questions about the purpose of a mission that had started as a humanitarian effort ten months earlier. Everyone knows the impact of seeing airliners crash into the World Trade Center.

Has CNN known the breadth and depth of their network's impact in both the Situation Room and the entire White House? Sol Levine answered that question. "We knew the Situation Room was watching us and we understood that there was a symbiotic relationship between us," Levine acknowledged.

Frank Sesno, who was not only a CNN White House correspondent, but also the CNN Washington bureau chief through 2001, said that he first became conscious that the Situation Room was watching CNN during the hijacking of a TWA airliner in 1985. "It was the first event in which we were able to bring real-time imagery to the White House. We quickly realized that our information was determinative in White House decision making."

Although cynics might suggest that CNN has become a subcontractor for the Situation Room, Frank Sesno said that the government never asked CNN to cover a story. "If an incident was that important, we would have been there on our own."

However, that possibility did not escape author Tom Clancy. In the first few pages of his 2000 book, *The Bear and the Dragon,* the author describes a scene that might portend the future of crisis alerting and reporting. Clancy wrote how someone mistakenly believed to be the head of the Russian security service had just been assassinated in Moscow:

> By this time, a CIA field officer named Tom Barlow was in the loop at the [American] embassy. The third-ranking spook in the current scheme of things, he didn't want to drive over to Dzerzhinskiy Square himself, but he did the next best thing. Barlow called the CNN office, the direct line to a friend.
>
> "Mike Evans."
>
> "Mike, this is Jimmy," Tom Barlow said, initiating a prearranged and much used lie. "Dzerzhinskiy Square, the murder of somebody in a Mercedes. Sounds messy and kind of spectacular."
>
> "Okay," the reporter said, making a brief note. "We're on it."
>
> At his desk, Barlow checked his watch. 8:52 local time. Evans was a hustling reporter for a hustling news service. Barlow figured there would be a mini-cam there in twenty minutes. The truck would have its own Ku-band uplink to a satellite, down from there to CNN Headquarters in Atlanta, and the same signal would be pirated by the DoD downlink at Fort Belvoir, Virginia, and spread around from there on government-owned satellites to interested parties.

Internet

Perhaps equal in significance to CNN in the Situation Room's alerting functions has been the Internet in recent years. Kevin Cosgriff brought an Internet capability to the Situation Room in the late 1990s.

"The impetus for installing an Internet terminal in the Situation Room initially came from a need to screen stories in major East Coast newspapers as early as possible, Cosgriff said. "Jim Steinberg, deputy national security adviser to President Clinton, was in Northern Ireland during the peace negotiations and didn't want to wait for the Situation Room to send him highlights from the printed versions of the *Washington Post* and the *New York Times.*" Cosgriff's duty officers found that the papers posted their big stories for the day on their Internet site much earlier than the delivery of the first editions at the White House. "Using the Internet, we could package the essentials from those stories then send them to Jim, giving him a heads-up five or six hours earlier than before. That way he got the news when he got up in the morning instead waiting until noon, London time."

Cosgriff built into the Situation Room's computer system the capability for the duty officer to switch from screening classified cables and messages to an Internet browser. "We not only started surfing the net for information relevant to the major issues of the day, but also anything associated with crises. Additionally, there was an increasingly relevant conversation on the Internet about major events and U.S. national security concerns that the normal news media outlets were not plugged into."

Cosgriff said that he wanted to add value to information that he sent to the President, instead of just giving him another piece of bad news. For example, if there was a major earthquake in another country, the duty officers could capture imagery posted on the Internet, gather information about nearby cities and economic infrastructure, or anything that might help them describe the impact of the disaster on the country.

4

COMMUNICATIONS

The President Is Calling

The creation of the Situation Room fundamentally changed the foreign policy process of the United States. Three political scientists, I. M. Destler, Leslie Gelb, and Anthony Lake, advanced this thesis in their 1984 book, *Our Own Worst Enemy*, an analysis of the making of U.S. foreign policy since World War II. They argued that the Situation Room and its communications systems helped presidents to seize control of the foreign policy system and thus create a true "operational presidency." The authors contended that the Situation Room "helped the NSC staff to serve the president as he must be served, even if it offered also unfair advantages in the bureaucratic competition." They affirmed that initially the Situation Room's communications systems brought Kennedy and his staff more fully into the policy game. They went on to state that those systems "would be employed by subsequent presidential aides—especially Kissinger and Brzezinski—to keep out State and Defense, sometimes even their Secretaries. The new communications networks allowed both presidents and White House staffers to get more deeply into the daily business of diplomacy, sometimes acting without the knowledge of the officials actually charged with those responsibilities. The machines have allowed the growth of the operational presidency."

The authors suggested that the operational presidency has markedly reduced the influence of the State Department in the creation and conduct of foreign policy. In their view, State's diminished role was not just a result of activism by the NSC and White House staff; it was largely from the capability of the White House to communicate directly with other governments through the use of Situation Room communications systems. In the old days, the State Department was the hub of a worldwide communications system that sent letters and cables to its embassies abroad containing carefully worded, precisely edited paragraphs that the ambassador was to pass to the host government. The recipient sent replies to those paragraphs to the State Department either through their embassy in Washington or back through the U.S. embassy. Dozens of people read each letter or cable.

It was the view of Lake and the others that the Situation Room's communications circuits allowed the White House to reach selectively into State's communications system—or, worse, from State's view, to bypass it altogether—and send a cable directly to a foreign head of state. Kennedy was apparently enamored with such an end run, which explains why he had the special telephone circuits to foreign heads of state installed in the Situation Room. Henry Kissinger established secret channels to the North Vietnamese in order to seek a negotiated end to the Vietnam War, as well as covert communications with the Chinese to initiate a dialogue between the two governments. President Carter's staff installed secure point-to-point teletype circuits with selected governments, and Carter used the Moscow Hot Line in an attempt to initiate a back channel dialogue with Soviet leader Leonid Brezhnev.

In an interesting bit of analysis, the three authors wrote that the operational presidency cut into State's influence much more than that of the Defense Department, the other major player in the foreign policy process. If the two giant bureaucracies were likened to factories, State would produce words; Defense, bullets. The President's staff could much more easily interpose itself in the world of words than it could in the realm of weapons systems.

Hal Saunders had the unique experience of working on the NSC staff from 1961 to 1974. He witnessed the impact of the new Situation Room on the Kennedy administration, then later watched Henry Kissinger use Sit Room communications systems in support of Nixon's initiatives. "Those of us on the staff realized that we needed to form our own policy framework, not to undercut State, but rather help the President ask the right questions," said Saunders.

Dr. Kissinger was particularly direct when I asked him about the impact of the Situation Room's communications systems on the presidency. "Given how the bureaucracies serve themselves, I think it is inconceivable that a modern president could succeed without independent access to information."

Brent Scowcroft, national security adviser to both Presidents Ford and George H. W. Bush, when asked about the Situation Room's role in defining the operational presidency, chose his words carefully. "In the sense that the Situation Room has allowed the President to receive information early, or at least simultaneously with his Cabinet agencies, then the Situation Room has been critical to the presidency."

Robert "Bud" McFarlane, who worked for both Nixon and Ford and was one of President Reagan's national security advisers, disagreed slightly with Lake's thesis. "The President's control of foreign policy is really a function of the larger role of the U.S. in world affairs after World War II," said McFarlane. "That increased role required the President to be in charge.

Also, the President's role depends on personalities. Once Richard Nixon and Henry Kissinger got to the White House, they wanted to centralize decision making at the White House. If there had not been a Situation Room then, they certainly would have created one."

Robert Gates, a career CIA official, who rose to become DCI, also served in several NSC staff positions, including deputy national security adviser to President George H. W. Bush. He agreed with the operational presidency thesis. "The Situation Room significantly enhanced the power of the presidency in the realm of foreign affairs," Gates said. "With this independent communications channel, the President and his national security adviser were no longer hostages to the agenda and institutional biases of the Secretaries of State and Defense, the Chairman of the Joint Chiefs, the DCI, and their minions. The agencies under those cabinet members often provided information as they saw fit, or even withheld information. The President was at their mercy regarding the detail of information or when he got it. The Situation Room changed all of that."

Nine years after the publication of *Our Own Worst Enemy*, Tony Lake became Bill Clinton's national security adviser. Was his thesis of the operational presidency still valid? Was the Situation Room still critical to the operational presidency? According to Lake:

> The operational presidency was inevitable. But my view of it changed. In 1984, we were not convinced that the White House should go beyond foreign policy formulation to its execution. We did not think the national security adviser need or should be personally involved in diplomacy. In retrospect, we were wrong.
>
> The role of the national security adviser in policy process is ever more central. Only the White House can adjudicate the

conflicting interests of the various departments. The issues facing us in a time of globalization increasingly affect the interests of many departments. And no one department will let another decide on such issues.

And when it comes to the conduct of diplomacy, I think there has been a trend that shows a decline in influence of the foreign ministries of major countries around the world. More countries are centralizing their foreign policy bureaucracies. There is therefore an increasing number of working relationships among national security advisers. They interact with themselves directly rather than through the traditional foreign ministry channels.

Given all that, then the national security adviser and the President need the Situation Room more now than in 1984.

The communications systems installed either directly in the Situation Room or in WHCA facilities for use by the Situation Room since 1961 are as varied as the challenges faced by the duty officers over the years. Central to this capability are the record communications circuits that connect the Situation Room to the vast networks managed by the State Department, the Pentagon, CIA, and other federal agencies that operate in the national security arena. They carry both routine and crisis traffic into the White House, originally by mechanical teletype machines, then later through computers. These systems have always met the Situation Room's needs, and both WHCA and NSC staff communications and computer specialists have steadily improved transmission speed and volume. They have been so reliable that they are boring, and nothing more really needs to be said about them.

However, there are other communications systems in the Situation Room that are more interesting and have colorful histories. First, there are voice systems. While a large number of calls are dialed directly, some are placed through two systems—the traditional White House switchboard, whose operators are renowned for their ability to find someone for the President, and the switchboard operated by WHCA. The Situation Room uses the WHCA system, known for years as "Signal" because WHCA used to be called the White House Signal Detachment, more often when reaching out into the national security community. WHCA also provides secure telephones that allow the duty officers, NSC staff, and the President to conduct classified conversations around the world. The President has mostly used Signal to conduct personal telephone calls to other heads of state, unless that leader's country had a dedicated, select communications line to the Situation Room.

Three presidents have directed that some of their telephone calls be taped. Kennedy's tapes of the Cuban Missile Crisis have enlightened historians and delighted both moviemakers and film fans. Johnson's tapes, which include many with nervous Situation Room duty officers, provide a wonderful insight into this complex man's mind. Nixon's tapes—well, we all know that story. More on taping presidential phone calls appears later in this chapter.

Second, there are "select" communications systems: dedicated, two-party circuits that connect the White House to selected countries. Traditionally they have been record communications versus voice and are used to send traffic to trusted allies, but special, secret agreements have added lines to other countries as well. Many have referred to some of these circuits as "back channel" systems, used with the most enthusiasm by Henry Kissinger during the Nixon administration. They were paths into other countries or entities through the back door; the front door was usually the State Department or our embassies.

Third, there is the Moscow "Hot Line," or as it is formally called, MOLINK, for MOscow LINK. While its main terminal is in the National Military Command Center in the Pentagon, a backup terminal is also manned by WHCA.

Fourth, the Situation Room has the capability to link the White House to other agencies, or even the President when he is traveling, via secure video teleconferencing. This communications feature expands the small conference room into a larger, virtual meeting room and has been a valuable tool during crises.

Last, the Situation Room was a leader in developing and installing secure facsimile communications systems. At first, during the Johnson administration, the Sit Room could exchange secure faxes with the other Washington operations centers. As the technology improved, secure fax systems proliferated to the point of ubiquity.

= = =

Telephone systems have been central to Situation Room operations from the beginning. The phones are always ringing. Although there has been a fairly constant, day-to-day level of phone activity over the years, there have also been spikes on top of those levels whenever there has been a "phone-friendly" president—Johnson, George H. W. Bush, and Clinton were the most active.

For years the duty officers, deputy director, and director of the Situation Room had large phone consoles covered with buttons. Several buttons accessed direct drops to the Signal switchboard, several others went directly to the White House operators. Others accessed outside lines assigned to the Situation Room. The Sit Room had direct lines upstairs to the national security adviser, his deputy, and the group of secretaries that worked for them. There were lines to the Secret Service and other specialized offices in the White House. There was a button labeled "The President."

When I became director, a communications technician explained the workings of my phone console and noted that there were two buttons I shouldn't touch. One was a direct line to the Soviet Embassy in Washington, the second to the Israeli

Embassy. He thought they were left over from the Nixon years and wasn't sure if they actually worked. As soon as I was alone, I punched one button; it rang, but no one answered. I accessed the second line and someone answered in a Slavic language. Unsure what to do next, I chickened out and hung up. I told the first WHCA technician I found to have the two lines disconnected immediately.

Bud McFarlane said that Kissinger used one of those direct lines several times during the 1973 Yom Kippur War. After the initial attack by Syria, Iraq, and Egypt, Israeli forces, led by Ariel Sharon, were driving hard toward Egypt and appeared intent on invading. "Henry reasoned that Sadat [Anwar Sadat was then president of Egypt] was essential to long-term peace, and if Sharon captured Cairo, Sadat would be humiliated and lose control of his country.

"Henry had sent several messages through the Israeli embassy in Washington, asking Golda Meir [then Israeli prime minister] to stop Sharon's advance, but had received no response," McFarlane said. "We were in the Situation Room when Henry picked up the phone and began exhorting the Israeli Ambassador. 'Jesus Christ, don't you understand?' Suddenly Henry stopped shouting and said, 'Oh.' I was later told that the Israeli calmly explained to Henry that his government might be more persuaded if he invoked a different prophet."

"I can't remember whether Sharon was the problem," Kissinger said with a smile when I retold McFarlane's story. "But I do recall that choice of words."

The national security adviser had a console only slightly less complicated than the duty officers, but had more direct lines to President and other senior White House staff. Most NSC staff members had phone sets that had at least one line to the White House operator and at least one regular outside line. In addition, they had a separate handset that connected them directly to the Signal switchboard.

The national security adviser, his deputies, most NSC staff members, and key Situation Room staff members had White House phones at home. I had a Signal handset on my nightstand and another in the basement. If the duty officer had to contact either the national security adviser or an NSC staffer at their home, he would ask Signal to ring up that person through his dedicated Signal line.

Lieutenant Commander Gerry McCabe had a phone at home during the early 1960s, and his widow, Joy Dell, said that the White House operator called her husband one night to complain about the McCabe children using the phone. "They were just little kids," said Mrs. McCabe forty years later. "They picked up the receiver and giggled when the operator answered."

The Situation Room also has elaborate secure telephone systems. In the 1960s and 1970s, they were crude and hard to use, mainly because there was no common system used throughout the government. Up through the Reagan administration, WHCA had a series of single-use contraptions to link the Situation Room with some of the off-the-beaten-path agencies. Secure calls were almost always routed through the WHCA switchboard and manually routed to the other end. There were separate handsets for the secure system. The President often kept his in a desk drawer and, although it was red, it was not a line to Moscow.

Selected NSC and White House staff members also had secure phones at home. Mine was a bulky and cranky STU-3 locked up in a safe in my basement. The duty officers first called me on the Signal line, because some things didn't need a classified introduction. When the situation called for secure communications, I walked down to the basement, opened the safe, pushed this, turned that, twisted twice, hoped for the best, and called them back. One Christmas Eve, I took my two sons and two of their cousins to the basement, activated the phone and put in a call to the North Pole. The forewarned Signal operator played Santa Claus and listened to the kids' wish list for Christmas.

During the Nixon administration, Henry Kissinger's assistant, Al Haig, asked Situation Room director David McManis to obtain a secure phone for Kissinger to use on a weekend trip to New York. There were few options in 1970, so McManis offered Kissinger only two choices. "I took WHCA's portable secure telephone up to Henry's office. I told him he could take it, hefting the forty-pound suitcase onto his desk, or, handing him a dime, use an equally secure system, a pay phone."

Unwanted callers occasionally got through to the Situation Room on the phone, and while most crank calls were a nuisance, some enlivened a slow night for the duty officers. The crank calls started immediately after the Situation Room opened for business. Chuck Enright recalled an incident in the early 1960s in which a man, claiming to be a friend of President Kennedy, wanted Enright to authorize the Passport Office in New York to issue the caller a passport. "I called the chief White House telephone operator, the President's personal secretary, several of the President's aides, and the Secret Service," wrote Enright in 1986. "None had heard of this fellow so I told him that I was sorry, but I couldn't help him. He told me that *I* would be the 'sorry one' the next day, but we never heard from him again."

Other callers claim to be foreign heads of state, but the duty officers always quiz them on current events, the structure of their alleged governments, and geography. One caller claimed to be the Israeli prime minister, but when we asked him to name the Israeli President, an office that is largely unknown to the public, he failed the quiz. Hard questions usually screened out the imposters, but there was always a chance that the caller was for real. Just in case, the Situation Room never connects the caller to the President, even if he seems real, but rather reports the call to the national security adviser. The President almost always never takes an incoming call, however valid, but rather calls back later.

The real Prince Charles of Britain did call at 2:00 one morning. David Sedney, a duty officer from State, recalled the incident. "The first three people who talked to Prince Charles thought it was a crank call—the White House telephone operator, her supervisor, and the senior duty officer. I asked him where he was and when he said 'New Zealand,' I thought that explained the odd hour of his call. We politely asked him pointed questions about the Windsor family and British history. When he answered everything correctly, we explained that we would coordinate with the British embassy in Washington and pass on his request to speak with the President to the national security adviser."

Until the widespread use of cellular phones in the 1990s, everyone carried a pager. While mine emitted a simple tone or vibration, David McManis, the director under Nixon, had a voice pager. "I was at back-to-school night, or something," recalled McManis, "and bang, the Signal operator came on the line and loudly announced: 'Mr. McManis, please call the White House.' The other parents were impressed."

In 1986, a duty officer paged me one snowy day in Washington to report yet another seizure of an American hostage in Lebanon, and I ended up in an uncomfortable situation. It was Sunday, and I was walking with my two boys toward the neighborhood sledding hill on the banks of the Potomac River. Although we had a mobile phone—we called it the Bat Phone in honor of the Masked Marvel—it was too cumbersome to use so I never carried it. I knocked on the door of a friend, Gene Gibbons, the White House correspondent for the Reuters news service and asked Gene if I could use his phone.

Midway through my conversation with the duty officer about the incident, I turned to Gene and said, "This is off the record, Gene, you can't use this to file a story." Gene smiled but carefully didn't make any promises.

The next morning I scanned the newswire reports about the kidnapping and found the Reuters story that I expected. Gene had filed the piece just minutes after I had left his kitchen, evidence that a good reporter uses every available source.

= = =

Presidential phone calls to other heads of state constituted one of the most demanding challenges to the Situation Room staff. One duty officer called a head-of-state call a "SweatEx," a sweat exercise; another said they were all-consuming and ate up a sizable chunk of the day.

Below are the general steps the Situation Room performs to set up and execute a head-of-state (HOS) call between the President and another head of state. For purposes of illustration, I'm using a hypothetical call between then–President Clinton and then–Russian President Boris Yeltsin.

1. The NSC executive secretary informs the Situation Room SDO that there will be a call to Yeltsin at a designated time.
2. The SDO notifies the senior director for Russian affairs on the NSC staff. The SDO then calls the designated contact in Moscow to determine if Yeltsin can speak with the President at the designated time.
3. The SDO calls the State Department Language Service to arrange for an interpreter to come to the Situation Room to assist in the call. The interpreter usually arrives in the Situation Room fifteen to twenty minutes before the scheduled call.
4. The senior director for Russian affairs sends a copy of the President's talking points to the Situation Room.
5. The SDO places the call to the established Kremlin tele-

phone number that Yeltsin commonly uses. Once Yeltsin comes on the line, the SDO introduces the President.

6. The Situation duty officers take verbatim notes of the conversation. Usually, one duty officer transcribes the President's remarks; another follows the other side of the conversation.

7. After the completion of the call, the Situation Room draws up a complete transcript of the conversation and submits it to the NSC executive secretary.

President Clinton and his staff entered office less organized than they later became. Neil O'Leary remembered trying to help them break their old campaign habits. "Clinton was used to just picking up a phone and calling someone," O'Leary said. "After the election, but before his inauguration, Clinton wanted us to set up calls to foreign leaders, but I declined because Bush was still the President." After the inauguration, when he was making get-acquainted calls to foreign leaders, O'Leary said Clinton and his staff still approached the whole thing rather informally, as they had done during the campaign.

"I asked Nancy Soderberg, a campaign aide who became the NSC staff secretary, if we could start using the tried-and-true method of making head-of-state calls that the Situation Room had been using for years," said O'Leary. "She said they would try it one time, but it had better work."

O'Leary said that the Situation Room set up the next call using the well-tested Situation Room protocol and things went great until midway through the conversation. "I had been monitoring the call along with my duty officers when I reached for something and accidentally pulled my telephone console off my desk," said O'Leary. "As it hit the floor, it cut off the President's conversation. As my career flashed before my eyes, we frantically got everyone reconnected and Nancy, who was steamed, was kind enough to give us another chance."

O'Leary said that his most memorable head-of-state call was between President Bush and Soviet President Mikhail Gorbachev on the occasion of the attempted overthrow of Gorbachev by disgruntled Communists in August 1991. Gorbachev, his wife, daughter, and son-in-law were vacationing at Cape Foros in the Crimea when on August 18 all of his communications were cut and a group from Moscow arrived to announce the coup d'état. On August 19, the coup leaders announced in Moscow that Gorbachev was ill and unable to perform as President. O'Leary recalled the next few days.

"As soon as we heard the news, President Bush wanted to try to get through to Gorbachev," recalls O'Leary. "We called our usual number in Moscow and I said, "President Bush wants to speak with President Gorbachev." A man at the other end stuttered and stammered, said he would be right back, and put the phone down. Moments later, he said Gorbachev was unavailable and hung up."

O'Leary tried again the next day and repeated his refrain, hoping to signal that the White House still considered Gorbachev to be the rightful head of state, but again, an uncertain voice announced that Gorbachev could not be reached. "But on the third day, we knew immediately that Gorbachev had regained control when the Kremlin operator was back to his businesslike and professional manner," said O'Leary, "and he quickly said that Gorbachev would soon be on the line. A cheer went up in the Sit Room as we relayed the news to the President."

Paul LeBras, who preceded O'Leary as director, said that the transition from Reagan to Bush was as interesting as the Bush-Clinton changeover.

"I learned quickly to never assume anything," said LeBras. "When Bush became President, one of the major changes in operations was the increase in the number of telephone calls Bush made to other heads of state. With Reagan, those calls were infrequent and we had about two days to get everything ready. But President Bush made them in bunches and with little notice."

LeBras said that one day he was told to prepare for five or six calls, one of them to President Botha of South Africa. "I was really surprised by that one, because I had nothing to indicate that we had anything cooking with South Africa," LeBras said. "Just to be sure, I went upstairs to see Brent Scowcroft's secretary. While she had told me Botha, she had actually mispronounced Pakistani Prime Minister Bhutto's name. I would have been toast if I had gotten Botha on the phone and had to tell him that President Bush didn't really want to talk to him."

LeBras also recalled an incident when he was unable to find an interpreter for a planned conversation between President Bush and King Juan Carlos of Spain. "I was getting a little frantic, but I found an NSC staff member who spoke Spanish. I explained the situation to him and asked for his help, but he said 'I don't do translations.' I appealed to the NSC executive secretary, who in turn convinced the man to help us. It was a close call."

Frank Sesno, a former CNN correspondent and bureau chief told me of an unusual precursor to a conversation between President George H. W. Bush and Turkish President Turgut Ozal during the Gulf War.

"Bush was returning from Camp David one day, and all of us in the news media were behind the rope line trying to ask questions," said Sesno. "Bush refused to comment, but he did say that he was headed inside the White House to call Ozal. John Sununu, Bush's chief of staff, told me later that when Ozal got on the line, he told Bush that he had been expecting the call because he had been watching CNN."

The duty officers have always monitored head-of-state phone calls in order to help produce a Memorandum of Conversation, a permanent record of the call for the NSC files. In some administrations, the cognizant NSC staff member drafted that memo; in others, the duty officers. In the controversy that swirled around President Clinton's last-minute pardons and commutations at the end of his second term, those "MEMCONs" received unusual attention.

Clinton discussed fugitive financier Marc Rich with Israeli Prime Minister Ehud Barak on three occasions in December 2000 and January 2001, and the Sit Room monitored those conversations. Congressional investigators investigating Clinton's surprising pardon of Rich gained access to the MEMCONs; *Newsweek* magazine described the conversations in August 2001. Could there have been tape recordings of the calls?

═ ═ ═

Alexander Butterfield told a congressional committee investigating the Watergate controversy in 1973 that President Nixon had installed a taping system to secretly record Oval Office conversations. The succeeding furor about a presidential cover-up of a "second-rate" burglary of a Washington office building ultimately led to Nixon's resignation. While the ensuing investigation into the tapes and their contents continued for a year, the immediate response by the Nixon White House to Butterfield's exposé was the cry that "other presidents had done the same thing."

Indeed, John Kennedy had installed a taping system, which produced recordings that became a valuable record of the Cuban Missile Crisis. Lyndon Johnson installed a much more elaborate taping system, including a Dictabelt recorder in the Situation Room. Most of Johnson's recordings were of telephone calls, and they constitute a sizable library, considering the man often made seventy-five to one hundred calls a day. Johnson specified that those tapes be kept from the public for fifty years after his death, but most are available for public playback at the LBJ Presidential Library in Austin, Texas.

Among the library's holdings is a collection of taped phone calls from Johnson to the Situation Room duty officer, usually made either right before he went to sleep at night or upon awakening early in the morning. The President gruffly asked pointed questions, and the tone of his voice made it clear to the young duty officers that he wanted a clear and exhaustive report with no how-do-you-do's. Most of the duty officers met the challenge, offering confident summaries of recent events, many of which covered the previous day's fighting in Vietnam. One or two of the duty officers sounded new to the job and their quavering voices were testimony to their inexperience in briefing a demanding President.

Johnson installed, in the Situation Room, a stand-alone recording device that was separate from the system he used to tape most of his phone calls. A Dictabelt recording machine, equipment commonly used by executives to dictate correspondence, captured a series of telephone conversations during the Dominican Crisis in 1965. The U.S. had dispatched troops to the Dominican Republic to restore order after a coup. In May of that year, Johnson's national security adviser, McGeorge Bundy, and Deputy Secretary of Defense Cyrus Vance traveled to the Dominican Republic in an attempt to broker an agreement between the hostile factions. Other Johnson advisers, Secretary of Defense Robert McNamara, chief of staff and press secretary Bill Moyers, and several others gathered in the Situation Room or the Cabinet Room to exchange phone calls with Bundy and Vance.

In later years, the Situation Room maintained a recording device to tape a dangerous-sounding crank call or, in rare occasions, a telephone conversation between the President and a foreign head of state. When I became director, we still had that capability, but we never taped either meetings or telephone calls while I was there. Under unfortunate circumstances, I discovered that, prior to my arrival, the duty officers occasionally taped a head-of-state call when no NSC staff member was on hand to help with the call or the watch team was shortedhanded. The duty officers used the tape to make sure their verbatim notes were accurate when drafting a written record of the conversation. They used ordinary tape cassettes and kept the used tapes in shoebox, rerecording over previous conversations.

But amid the scandal-mongering and speculation that followed the exposure of Ollie North's Iran-Contra enterprise, the frenzied news media was seeking Watergate parallels and found its way to the "secret" Situation Room taping system. Our shoebox was exposed to the hard, cold light of day.

The *Washington Post's* Bob Woodward wrote a front-page article on December 19, 1986, that carried the headline, "White House Taping System Disclosed, Computer and Audio Recordings May Contain Data on Iran Deal." Seemingly eager to find information analogous to the Nixon tapes that helped unravel the Watergate cover-up, Woodward wrote that "the high quality taping system in the White House Situation Room was used to record some of President Reagan's key foreign policy meetings, according to one source with firsthand knowledge." Woodward went on to report that Reagan held several key meetings in the Situation Room regarding the secret Iran initiative and that Ollie North used the Situation Room as a second office. Citing "informed sources," Woodward suggested that there might be tapes that would shed light on the "secret Iran arms affair." Woodward also wrote about the NSC email system, "PROFS," which did indeed keep a record of emails between North, Bud McFarlane, and John Poindexter; that record became central to the following investigation. But the lead on the secret telephone recording system and secretly taped presidential meetings turned out to be an investigative dry hole.

I inventoried the shoebox on the day Woodward's story appeared and found about a dozen tapes. Most were of Reagan calls to heads of state, and the rest were recordings of other, miscellaneous telephone conversations.

We did have fittings installed in the top of the table in the conference room that accepted microphones. We never used them while I was director, and if we had, the microphones would have been in plain sight. Regarding telephone calls, all we had was a few old tapes and none of the conversations were related to Iran-Contra. Sure, Ollie spent a lot of time in the Situation Room, but we never recorded his calls. The Press Office threw all the facts out to the news media in the few days that followed Woodward's piece and the controversy quickly dissipated. The Iran-Contra special prosecutor later seized the tapes, and my boss told me to not record any more heads-of-state calls. None has been since.

=== === ===

"I told Kissinger and Haig that if they told me where they wanted a message sent and whom they didn't want to see it as it passed through the U.S. communications system, I would find a way to get it there," said former Situation Room director David McManis. "As time passed, I somewhat regretted that offer, since, as an intelligence professional, I was subverting the system."

Henry Kissinger accepted McManis's offer and frequently used the specialized communications systems available through the Situation Room during his years as the national security adviser to President Nixon. Whether Kissinger became the master of secret, back channel negotiations because of the Sit Room's capabilities, or the Sit Room adapted to Kissinger's style is arguable. Nevertheless, the best example of Kissinger's use of the Situation Room to conduct secret diplomacy was his early, covert negotiations with the North Vietnamese, which ultimately led to the Paris peace talks to end the war in Vietnam. McManis, Kissinger's Sit Room director, described the beginnings of the peace talks.

"Henry wanted a completely secure, watertight means of communicating with Dick Walters in Paris, who he asked to be the go-between with the North Vietnamese," said McManis. (Lieutenant General Vernon "Dick" Walters was the defense attaché at the U.S. embassy in Paris, and President Nixon trusted him implicitly.) "Kissinger and Haig did not want to even use CIA channels to Paris, so they asked me to devise a means of secure comms with Walters. My only solution was to use a one-time pad."

A one-time pad is one of the most secure means of encrypting a written message. While it is simple and secure, encoding and decoding long messages were laborious projects. Conceptually, a one-time pad is nothing more than pad of paper with each sheet in the pad containing a coding algorithm that is to be used only once—tear a sheet from the pad, use it to encode a message, then throw it away. For example, if one sheet has an encoding sequence which converts the letter "a" to the letter "k," then only those people who have a copy of the corresponding sheet from the pad can change "k" back to "a." The receiver also discards the sheet after decoding the message.

Haig sent McManis to Europe to deliver a one-time pad to Dick Walters so Kissinger could start sending messages to the North Vietnamese through Walters. But first, McManis stopped in Brussels to organize the logistics of covert air travel between Washington and Paris.

"I took off from New York, first class by the way, with two one-time pads under my shirt," said McManis. "Haig instructed me to meet with General Andy Goodpaster, the Army officer in charge of U.S. forces in Europe as well as the supreme commander of NATO forces. We needed Goodpaster's help to get U.S. military aircraft into Europe without notice. I taught him how to use the one-time pad, but he was skeptical, almost to the point of annoyance, of its actual employment." Once in

Paris, Walters, according to McManis, was more receptive to the use of the one-time pad. He also was a gracious host to McManis, putting up David in his Paris apartment.

As Andy Goodpaster suggested, Kissinger rarely used the one-time pads to communicate with Walters. Instead, he simply sent McManis, or one of David's staff to Paris with messages for Walters. "Kissinger and Haig did not even trust the Armed Forces Courier system, so they sent either me or my deputy, Jim Fazio, to Paris," said McManis. "Later, we started asking the duty officers to make trips to share the load, and, between all of us, we made about two dozen trips to Paris. I asked everyone to keep his passport in the Sit Room because sometimes Haig would walk in with a briefcase and ask someone to fly to Paris right then. Once, when I was on vacation, Jim sent a duty officer who came to work that day without any money; Al called Walters and asked him to spot the duty officer some meal money."

Walters asked duty officer Jim Middleton on one trip to take back a cosmetic case the general's sister had left at his residence in Paris. Jim had almost no other luggage, since the turnaround time was short. He agreed, but when he got to U.S. Customs in New York, the agent wanted to see what was inside—perfume, lipstick, powder, and so on. Middleton wasn't sure how he was going to explain, and finally muttered the well-known, "You aren't going to believe this . . ." to the official, who smiled and raised an eyebrow, but let him go.

When Nixon decided to make secret contact with the Chinese in preparation for both his landmark trip to China and diplomatic relations, Kissinger called on the Situation Room to help establish covert communications with the Chinese mission at the United Nations in New York City.

"Haig gave me a briefcase one evening, along with instructions on where to take it and who I should give it to," said McManis. "I flew to New York on the Eastern shuttle, took a taxi to Times Square, then walked circuitously to a nondescript brownstone. I wore the requisite trench coat and hat, and childhood dreams of spies and secret meetings flashed through my mind. A young woman served me tea while I handed over the package from Henry.

"I made a lot of trips to New York carrying messages to the Chinese, and it seemed like all were at night and it was always raining," said McManis. "Also, I assumed that the FBI had a surveillance unit in a building across the street, so I began to worry that I might be called back to NSA headquarters for questioning—'What are you doing at the Chinese mission in New York?' I quickly told, in general terms, Dr. Tordella, NSA's deputy director, about my travels."

"President Nixon's China initiative was a good example of the usefulness of back channel communications," said Al Haig. "Our opening of relations with China would still be a matter of debate today if we had not explored the early contact with the Chinese through back channels. Since the government leaks like a sieve, word of Nixon's intentions would have gotten to all the vested interest groups, especially the Taiwan lobby, and they might have attempted to derail the initiative."

Johnathan Howe, who served on the NSC staff several times during his career in the Navy, worked there first as a military assistant to Kissinger during the early Nixon years and recalled his experiences with the Situation Room. "We really depended on the Situation Room in those days," said Howe. "Henry and President Nixon had all those secret initiatives under way and Henry did not want to use the bureaucracy at State or even the rest of the NSC staff for fear of leaks, so we sought logistics support from Sit Room staff. Not only did the Situation Room perform all of their normal duties, they also helped us establish and operate a large number of back channel communications links."

Walt Rostow, Johnson's national security adviser, told me

that President Johnson had considered contacting French Premier Charles de Gaulle in 1968 through back channels when the French leader, who many thought arrogantly kept his own counsel, was besieged by domestic riots. "I told Johnson that he could try, but that it wasn't likely that de Gaulle would listen to him or anyone else."

The existence of special circuits between the Situation Room and foreign governments has been a source of tension between the White House and the State Department, the agency that is nominally in charge of communications between the United States and other nations. Duty officer David Sedney found himself a victim of that tension. "I hand-carried to State a particularly sensitive document that Scowcroft wanted Secretary of State Baker to see," said Sedney. "When I delivered the package to a deputy executive secretary at State, the man who had been my boss before I went to the Sit Room, he asked if the White House had received the document via any of our 'special means.' I felt quite uncomfortable, but I had to decline to answer his question." Luckily, Sedney weathered that inquisition and went on to a successful career as a Foreign Service officer.

All administrations have felt that it was important to be able to reach selected countries through back channels. The countries served by them are rarely identified, and the circuits have been sensitive issues because if third parties became aware of selective communications agreements, they might feel slighted that they had not been accorded the same level of confidential communications.

= = =

"Mr. President, the Hot Line is up!"

That's how Secretary of Defense Robert McNamara greeted President Lyndon Johnson on the telephone at 7:30 A.M. on June 5, 1967. Just three hours earlier, Johnson's national security adviser, Walt Rostow, had also called Johnson to alert the

President that Israel was at war with Syria and Egypt. Soviet Premier Alexei Kosygin activated the Hot Line between Washington and Moscow to register Soviet concerns about the hostilities. Installed between the capitals of the two major cold war participants in 1963, the communications link, called MOLINK in the U.S., had never been used except for testing.

McNamara, in an oral history for the Johnson Presidential Library, said:

> I was called that morning by the duty officer in the War Room of the Pentagon. He told me that Prime Minister Kosygin wished to talk to President Johnson on the Hot Line and what response should he, the duty officer, make. I didn't understand why the duty officer was asking me, [because] that was a White House decision. Much to my surprise, the duty officer explained that the Hot Line terminated in the Pentagon, not the White House.
>
> "General, [McNamara was speaking to the duty officer] we are spending forty billion dollars a year on the defense budget, can't you take a few thousand of those dollars and get these goddamn lines patched across the river to the White House? You call the Situation Room and I'll call the President and we'll decide what to do."
>
> I then called the President, knowing he probably would be asleep. An Air Force sergeant who was close to his room, answered the telephone and said that the President was asleep and didn't like to be awakened. I told the sergeant that I knew that but go tell the President that Bob McNamara is on the line and asked that he be awakened. The sergeant did and the President came to the phone and in a sleepy, gruff voice said, "Goddamn it, Bob, what is the problem?" "Well," I said, "Mr. President, Prime Minister Kosygin wishes to talk with you. What should I say?"

McNamara said that Johnson was shocked and surprised and said:

"What do you think I should say?"

I said, "I think you should say that you'll be available for consultations with him in twenty minutes." The President said to me, "You tell him that and, in the meantime, you get yourself and Dean Rusk [Secretary of State] over here and we'll meet in the Situation Room."

The U.S. and the Soviet Union activated the MOLINK in 1963, but as McNamara discovered, the military ran the U.S. end of the link. The Pentagon later formalized the quick, temporary patch to connect the Situation Room with the MOLINK by installing an ancillary terminal, complete with military operators, in the WHCA communications (comms) center in the East Wing basement. The comms center sent MOLINK messages to the Situation Room, not only in 1967, but also for several years after, by pneumatic tube until computer processors were installed in the communications center and the Sit Room. The link has always been for record communications: first teletype, later computer-to-computer, with a FAX capability. There has never been a voice line with a red telephone on the President's desk.

Nineteen other MOLINK exchanges between Washington and Moscow followed that initial message from the Soviets during the Six-Day War in 1967. Llewellyn Thompson, the U.S. Ambassador to the Soviet Union, was in Washington during that brief week of fighting and joined the near continual meetings in the Situation Room. In a 1968 account of the MOLINK exchanges, Thompson recalled that the Soviet side made quite a point that President Johnson be physically present at the U.S. end of the line before they started the exchange.

"President Johnson's first message to Kosygin was actually addressed to 'Comrade Kosygin,'" Thompson said. "Apparently, the American Hot Line operators asked the Moscow operators what was the proper way to address Kosygin. They got back the answer, 'Comrade Kosygin,' and so the message went." Later, Thompson talked with Soviet Ambassador to the U.S., Anatoly Dobrynin, who had been on the Moscow end of the line during the Six-Day War, about the unusual salutation. "The Russians wondered if the President was making a joke, or making fun of them in some way," said Thompson. "However, Dobrynin said he guessed how it had happened."

The exchanges on the MOLINK that week were so frequent that Johnson and his advisers remained in the Situation Room for hours at a time. Walt Rostow said that Johnson was not trying to run the crisis from the Situation Room, but staying there was easier than running up and down the stairs to the Oval Office. On June 8, for example, the Soviets sent messages at 9:48 A.M. and 12:20 P.M., and Johnson sent messages to them at 11:00 A.M., 11:35 A.M., and 3:36 P.M. Rostow described the process:

> When a Soviet message came in, the comms center sent the Cyrillic text over to the Situation Room by pneumatic tube. Some one, maybe Art McCafferty [the Situation Room director] or Thompson undertook a quick translation so we could start talking with the President about what it meant and how to reply. Rusk and McNamara were there, along with Mac Bundy, who Johnson invited for his advice, and Clark Clifford [then head of the President's Foreign Intelligence advisery board]. Once we had a complete translation, my secretary, Lois Nivens, typed up the formal message and passed copies around the table.

Rostow said that once they had discussed the Soviet message, they decided if and what the reply should be. "Someone started drafting our message, often President Johnson," Rostow said. "Lois then typed our reply and passed out copies for all to double-check the wording. I'm glad we never used the telephone or we might have inadvertently said the wrong thing. I then sent the outgoing message back to the comms center for transmission."

On June 8, 1967, during the Six-Day War, the Israelis attacked a U.S. Navy intelligence-gathering ship, USS *Liberty*, with aircraft and torpedo boats. The attack severely damaged the ship, killed thirty-four of the crew, and wounded two-thirds of the remainder. As ships of the U.S. Sixth Fleet rushed to *Liberty's* assistance, Johnson immediately sent a MOLINK message to Kosygin informing him of the attack. He explained that the movement of U.S. ships did not represent U.S. involvement in the Arab-Israeli war, but rather assistance to the *Liberty* and protection against further attack. Ambassador Thompson later justified this use of the Hot Line: "We were using it the right way, to prevent a danger of war arising out of misunderstanding. The message made a big impression on the Russians."

Joe Shergalis was a duty officer during the Six-Day War and he remembered the electricity in the Sit Room when Moscow sent a message on the Hot Line. "We had a special phone to the Pentagon terminal and when the Soviets activated the Hot Line, the operators called us with a heads-up," said Shergalis. "The hair on the back of my neck stood up because I knew something really important was about to happen."

In a 1988 article in the *New York Times Magazine,* Webster Stone wrote that impetus for a direct link between Moscow and Washington came from Jess Gorkin, editor of *Parade Magazine.* Gorkin published an open letter to both President Eisenhower and the Soviet Secretary General Nikita Khrushchev, in which Gorkin urged the two leaders to establish a Hot Line. Gorkin even badgered the 1960 presidential candidates, Nixon and Kennedy, about the need for a communications link. The State and Defense Departments reportedly objected to the proposal, fearing the President would talk to their counterparts behind their backs.

The idea of a Moscow Hot Line gained considerable momentum after the Cuban Missile Crisis in October 1962. Messages between Kennedy and Khrushchev took anxious hours to travel through normal diplomatic communications links, and both sides released their statements to the news media to speed transmission times.

In May 1963, representatives from the U.S. and the Soviet Union met in Geneva, Switzerland, to begin technical discussions aimed at establishing a direct link between the two countries. At an eighteen-nation disarmament conference in Geneva during June 1963, the U.S. and the Soviets signed an agreement to establish direct communications between their respective capitals. On July 13, 1963, the U.S. sent communications equipment to Moscow for their terminal, via U.S. Ambassador Averell Harriman's plane. On August 20, Soviet equipment arrived in Washington. On August 30, 1963, the two countries activated the Washington-Moscow Hot Line with test messages.

Two circuits initially connected a single U.S. terminal in the Pentagon's National Military Command Center to the Kremlin. The primary cable circuit reached Europe via a transatlantic undersea cable to London, then through Copenhagen, Stockholm, and Helsinki to Moscow. A coordinating circuit was a radio teletype channel via Tangiers, in North Africa, to Moscow. The two terminals sent periodic test messages to each other to keep the line open. The U.S. received all Soviet messages in Russian; U.S. messages were printed out in English. In 1984, the two countries upgraded the MOLINK from a teletype circuit to a computer-driven link. The operators established new communications pathways also, using two communications satellites.

The two countries have used the MOLINK sparingly in the

years since the 1967 Six-Day War. Nixon used it twice, once during the Yom Kippur War in 1973. President Carter used it to send a personal letter to Soviet leader Leonid Brezhnev, reportedly on arms control issues. Dennis Chapman, then director of the Situation Room recalled the incident.

"Brzezinski asked me how to send a Hot Line message, so I pulled out our little book with all the instructions. The message Carter wanted to send didn't really meet the established criteria for MOLINK messages, but Brzezinski insisted on using it. Later, the news media reported that the Soviets were upset with Carter for using the Hot Line for nonemergency matters, which the Soviets reportedly felt was an improper use of the link. Carter did use it, however, to send a strong objection to the Soviets regarding their invasion of Afghanistan."

With the disintegration of the Soviet Union and the rise in personal diplomacy, the significance of the MOLINK has waned a bit. After Reagan, both Presidents Bush and Clinton did not hesitate to pick up a regular phone and call Mikhail Gorbachev, Boris Yeltsin, or Vladimir Putin.

There is also a "warm line" between Moscow and Washington at the Nuclear Risk Reduction Center (NRRC) in each city. Established in 1987, the NRRC in Washington is managed by the State Department and supplements both traditional diplomatic channels and the MOLINK. The State Department describes the NRRC as "part of an increasingly complex system of confidence- and security-building measures designed to reduce the risk of war and to promote arms control and stability in the current post Cold War climate." In addition to Russia, Belarus, Ukraine, and Kazakhstan are part of the NRRC system, and each has direct communications links with the NRRC at State.

I, too, felt like Bob McNamara when one of my duty officers called me late one night in 1986 to announce that the Hot Line was up, and a message from Gorbachev to President Reagan was coming out of the printer at the MOLINK terminal in the East Wing basement. Moscow sent the letter via the MOLINK fax—it was thirteen pages long, handwritten, and in Russian.

I called John Poindexter, Reagan's national security adviser, and briefed him on this unexpected event. He surmised that Gorbachev's message was in response to a handwritten letter that Reagan had sent to Gorbachev via diplomatic pouch. I offered to send a copy of the letter to State for translation, but Poindexter said, in effect, "Not so fast." "I don't want State reading that letter until we know what it says," he told me. "Can you get it translated?" he asked.

I told him that I thought that the Russian linguists assigned to the MOLINK terminal in the East Wing basement could take a crack at it, but they were trained in the Russian used in military matters rather than in high diplomacy. Poindexter agreed and asked that the operators call him as they worked their way through the message.

The two young men began the laborious translation process, taking about an hour a page in the beginning. They were challenged not only by Gorbachev's idiosyncratic Russian, but also by his handwriting. They called Poindexter on a secure phone as they finished each page, and by the daily NSC staff meeting in the Situation Room the next morning, the operators had a fair translation ready. Jack Matlock, the senior director on the NSC staff for Soviet matters, and later Ambassador to Moscow, quibbled over some of the translation, but the gist of Gorbachev's letter was clear.

— — —

Late in the Reagan administration, we expanded the video teleconferencing capabilities of the Situation Room, adding a new dimension to interagency coordination and crisis management. Although the Situation Room had a video link with the NMCC for several years, the new system allowed for more participants. The NSC staff under George H. W. Bush used the new equipment system frequently, especially during the Gulf War, as has each succeeding administration.

Bob Gates, deputy national security adviser to President George H. W. Bush, said that the secure video teleconferencing system was extraordinarily valuable during crises. "It was a truly useful high-tech development," Gates said. "First, it helped avoid the parade of black cars outside the West Wing which was a dead give-away to the press that something was up. Secondly, it allowed each member of the Principals and Deputies committees to stay at home during crisis coordination meetings and sit on top of his own information stovepipe. When everyone meets in the Situation Room, the attendees are cut off from their respective institutions and all the information that is unique to those agencies.

"I thought the video conferences were not that useful for routine policy meetings because one never knew who was standing off-camera at the other sites," said Gates. "Also, some users had trouble adjusting to the procedures—they kept looking in their own monitors to fix their tie or comb their hair."

An interesting employment of video conferencing in the Situation Room was a remarkable bit of electronic diplomacy arranged in February 2000 between President Clinton and the participants of the Burundi peace talks in Arusha, Tanzania. Nelson Mandela led a delegation that attempted to mediate between warring factions in the East African nation of Burundi. Gayle Smith, senior director of African Affairs on the NSC staff, said that Clinton had wanted to attend the talks in Arusha, but was unable to because of scheduling conflicts. So Smith enlisted the help of the Situation Room and WHCA to set up a video link between the White House and Arusha.

"The President, Secretary Albright, and Sandy Berger sat in the Sit Room and spoke directly to representatives of the Burundi government, the opposition, and Mandela," said Smith. "The President's message had a powerful effect, just as if he had been there. It was a historic and valuable use of modern communications."

The Clinton administration not only brought African politicians into the Situation Room through videoconferencing, but also, in a very rare instance, the American public. In September 1997, the public interest cable network C-SPAN requested the opportunity to initiate a live broadcast from the White House to mark the fiftieth anniversary of the establishment of the National Security Council. P. J. Crowley, the NSC press spokesman, arranged for the cameras to be set up in the Situation Room, with Sandy Berger's permission. C-SPAN brought in Zbigniew Brzezinski, President Carter's national security adviser, and Alexander Haig, former Secretary of State under Reagan and an NSC aide to Henry Kissinger under Nixon, to join Berger in the Situation Room for the show.

"Brzezinski and Haig made remarks and answered questions from viewers for the first thirty minutes," said Crowley. "The first question to Brzezinski was something about his reaction to appearing on TV in the Sit Room. Brzezinski replied that, 'If I were still the national security adviser, this wouldn't be happening!' I laughed and so did Al Haig, who told Brzezinski to lighten up." Later when Berger joined them for the last half of the show, he said he was pleased that C-SPAN was there and was glad that the viewers had a chance to see the room where so much history had been made over the years.

President George W. Bush found the videoconferencing system useful in the immediate aftermath of the terrorist attacks on the World Trade Center in New York and the Pentagon on September 11, 2001. He used the system to contact his advisers in Washington while he was in Omaha, Nebraska, on the day of the attacks, then later to communicate with the rest of his National Security Council while he was at Camp David on the weekends.

On November 12, 2001, an American Airlines passenger jet

crashed in Queens, N.Y., shortly after takeoff. Tom Ridge, President Bush's Homeland Security director, immediately went to the Situation Room and initiated a secure video teleconference with several agencies to exchange information about the crash and assess its possible causes.

Jim Steinberg, deputy national security adviser to Bill Clinton, used the Sit Room's video teleconferencing system frequently during Clinton's second term. "I took a mobile video unit with me when I traveled so I could continue to attend Deputies meetings," said Steinberg. "In fact, it was especially useful on a trip to South America with President Clinton. TV coverage of the World Series was hard to find, so we asked the Sit Room to patch the broadcast into the Washington end of the videoconferencing circuit, then send it to us. About twenty-five of our traveling party crowded into a small room to watch the sixth game of the series."

= = =

When Art McCafferty formed the Washington Area Operations and Command Center Committee (WAOCCC) in the 1960s, his major goal was to foster improved coordination between agencies during crises. But he also used the group to help develop a secure facsimile communications system. The WAOCCC sponsored the creation of the Washington LDX network—Long Distance Xerography—and soon the Defense Communications Agency built and installed terminals in the Situation Room, at State, Defense, CIA, NSA, and DIA. The terminals were huge by today's standards, complete with a bulky steel cabinet, heavy doors, and special crypto gear; they looked like they should have been on the bridge of a battleship. But the LDX revolutionized the once-staid art of paper shuffling in Washington. State desk officers zapped their carefully worded paragraphs to the NSC staff for review, and soon directives and memos swiftly found their way into all corners of the federal bureaucracy. A later version of the secure facsimile system was called WASHFAX.

"Henry Kissinger loved new technology, especially the new LDX," recalled former duty officer Joe Shergalis. "Kissinger brought the Soviet Ambassador, Anatoly Dobrynin, into the Sit Room one evening to show off the LDX. The machine had a test feature which made it act like a regular Xerox, so Kissinger had us insert a page in one side and Dobrynin watched a copy come out the other."

"I don't remember showing Drobrynin the LDX, but I did escort him down to the Situation Room," Kissinger said. "I wanted to show him where I held meetings. He could then boast to Moscow that he had access to the White House and I hoped that would improve both his standing and our channel of communications."

Secure facsimile systems improved to the point that, by the Reagan years, WHCA carried a portable system wherever the President traveled. We faxed the daily intelligence summaries to Reagan's ranch, and the military aide on duty picked up the papers at the WHCA comms shack and delivered the package to the President. Camp David and Air Force One were equipped with secure faxes. Wherever the President traveled, a miniature blizzard of paper followed close behind.

The staff of the Situation Room began to move toward electronic file transfer during the Clinton administration. Kevin Cosgriff said that the Situation Room joined other modern government and business enterprises on the information highway and gradually moved away from just faxing paper. They began to electronically swap files, send PDF documents instead of faxes, and electronically transfer previously pure paper intelligence reports between the Sit Room and the other agencies. The duty officers can now make files available to remote terminals, significantly enhancing support for traveling presidents and their staff.

The Situation Room generally has stayed abreast of communications developments through the years, but its record has been uneven. The LDX, for an example, represented leading-edge technology, but the regular phone system lagged behind private industry in the 1980s. When it has fallen behind, it is often because the federal government is not nimble enough to rapidly incorporate new communications technology into daily operations. Until the 1990s, the Situation Room did not have its own information systems support staff and had to depend on WHCA for not only communications support, but also for computer systems development and operation. In the 1980s, the computer wizards in the Crisis Management Center dramatically upgraded the Sit Room systems, and that group grew into the current support staff.

5

THE CONFERENCE ROOM

Meetings in the Woodshed

"Henry is going to take the CIA to the woodshed. Do you want to join us?"

Tony Lake, President Clinton's first national security adviser, recalled the moment when Al Haig asked him that question shortly after Lake joined the NSC staff early in the Nixon administration. At that time, Haig was an assistant to Henry Kissinger. "Henry was arguing with CIA about how the Soviet Union intended to use the SS-9, one of their new intercontinental ballistic missiles," Lake said. "Al invited me to attend a meeting with Henry and a CIA analyst in the conference room in the Situation Room. I was so naive that during the weeks that followed the meeting, I referred to the conference room as the 'woodshed' . . . I thought that was its name!"

Henry Kissinger's old woodshed is a small conference room within the Situation Room complex in the basement of the White House West Wing. It is one of several rooms in the complex that has evolved since 1961. The complex, even though the NSC has enlarged the facility moderately over the years, remains distinctly small and cramped when compared with other operations centers in either the federal government or private industry.

Interestingly, despite the thousands of references to the Situation Room by the news media during the past forty years, so few people have ever visited the Situation Room that public perceptions of the facility are largely shaped by the entertainment industry. Compared with the huge war room in the 1960s film, *Doctor Strangelove,* or the set in the current popular TV series, *The West Wing,* the actual conference room remains disappointingly small and relatively low-tech. Why the Situation Room has yet to meet Hollywood's expectations is a good story.

= = =

When Tazewell Shepard, Kennedy's naval aide, built the Situation Room in 1961, there were four small rooms: the conference room, a file storage room that doubled as a rear-projection booth for the conference room, a small space for the duty officer, and an office for the first officer-in-charge, Lieutenant Commander Gerry McCabe, USN.

In 1961, the conference room was clearly the only room in the White House decorated in the Danish-modern style favored by many residential and commercial designers of the day. The table was polished wood with clean, simple lines and straight legs. Around it were eight chairs with molded plywood legs and curved backs and armrests that reflected standard contemporary designs. Shepard's Seabees covered the walls with the same type of wood paneling that many suburbanites were hanging in the basements of their new homes in nearby Fairfax County, Virginia. A large Mercator projection map of the world covered one wall and floor-to-ceiling draperies hid the rear-projection screen and a large, cork bulletin board. An unsubstantial aluminum podium, covered with imitation wood-grain vinyl, stood near the end of the conference table. Contemporary, bullet-shaped spotlights hung from the ceiling to illuminate the maps, and there were two black, rotary telephones on a small table along one wall. Large, government-issue glass ashtrays on the table reflected one of the habits of the day.

The file and storage room was adjacent to one wall of the conference room. In addition to the filing shelves, a movie projector and an old lantern slide projector were mounted on a large stand. Both were used to project images on the frosted-glass rear projection screen mounted in the wall common to the file and conference rooms.

Adjacent to the conference room was a small office for the duty officer. Initially, the room had two desks and a table for the newswire printers. Commander McCabe's office was also next to the conference room. He had a seven-foot, polar projection map of the world on one wall, a bulletin board for smaller maps on another, acoustical tile on the wall nearest the White House Mess, and, of course, some of that rec room paneling. His desk was a large, wooden VIP model with an executive-style, navy-blue leather chair. He had hung an autographed photo of the Chief of Naval Operations, Admiral Arleigh "31 Knot" Burke, on one wall just next to the door leading to a secure storage vault.

In July 1965, Art McCafferty, who became the first full-fledged director of the Situation Room upon Kennedy's assassination, sought to expand the Situation Room complex to accommodate planned upgrades of its communications systems. He needed space for three new systems—the new LDX, the secure fax that became so important to all Washington operations centers; a new-generation secure telephone system; and a more secure teleconferencing system. McCafferty estimated that a new 1,500-square-foot space would cost $153,000, but he would need another $350,000 to relocate other offices in the West Basement in order to preclude new construction outside the existing basement walls. Apparently that request was too large, because Marvin Watson, President Johnson's chief of staff, approved only the construction of a shielded communications enclosure as an addition to the Situation Room. With Watson's approval, the General Services Administration awarded the job to the lowest bidder at a cost of $28,000. Mc-George Bundy thought that total was a bit high, but wrote, "[L]ife is too short and we should proceed with the low bid."

The conference room remained generally unchanged through the Johnson years; pictures taken of LBJ and his advisers during the 1967 Six-Day War revealed the same paneling and maps. New ceiling light fixtures had been added for more light.

David McManis, who became the director in 1969 after several years as the NSA liaison officer, recalled Nixon passing through the Situation Room on an orientation tour. "He was not pleased with the facility," said McManis. "He turned to his staff and told them to 'do something about this place.'" Soon McManis and Brigadier General Jack Albright, WHCA's commander, began to plan a dramatic upgrade to the Situation Room. They developed building plans and obtained a promise for funding—$500,000 from the Defense Communications Agency, which supported much of WHCA's activities. McManis remembers that they had big plans.

"It was a grand scheme. We wanted to dig up the South Lawn and build an underground complex to rival the room in *Doctor Strangelove.* We envisioned four underground levels, two for the comms equipment and computers, one for a conference room, and the top floor for the duty officers."

Nixon approved the construction of a new Situation Room complex and DCA's contractor had started test borings of the South Lawn when the federal government announced a freeze on new construction projects. "I suspect we might have gotten around the freeze," recalled McManis over thirty years later. "But it's my guess that Haldeman and Erlichman, Nixon's chief domestic advisers, viewed the new Situation Room as the main jewel in Henry Kissinger's empire and they might have lobbied for complete adherence to the freeze."

McManis said they used some of the funding approved for the new facility to upgrade and renovate the existing spaces in the Situation Room. They installed the polished cherry wood table and paneling that remained until the late 1990s in the conference room, bought new chairs and carpet, and changed the interior decoration. The Situation Room staff collaborated with WHCA to develop a computer-based processing system for the incoming and outgoing cable traffic. Previous crises— the Six-Day War, the Soviet invasion of Czechoslovakia, and the North Korean shootdown of a Navy reconnaissance air- craft—overwhelmed the old, almost manual system. The new system allowed McManis's duty officers to screen an incoming message on a terminal video screen, then direct its dissemina- tion—printing, filing, or forwarding—through keyboard strokes. That process, albeit with far more powerful PCs and computer workstations, continues today.

Walt Rostow, deputy national security adviser to Kennedy when the Situation Room was built in 1961, made a prophetic statement in 1969 after hearing from Dave McManis about the cancelled underground project. "He told me that if we had dug a big hole with blast-proof door, no one would ever use it," said McManis. Later in the early 1980s, the NSC staff built a large Crisis Management Center in what was then the Old Execu- tive Office Building next door to the White House. After a few years, no one used it either.

During the Ford administration, the NSC staff slightly in- creased the size of the complex and added a back door. The White House had previously covered over the indoor swim- ming pool in the West Terrace that Kennedy and Johnson en- joyed and converted the space to the White House press briefing theater. The White House then built an outdoor pool on the South Lawn just south of the Oval Office. Initially, if the President and his family, starting with Ford, wanted to take a dip, they had to walk outside from the mansion to the pool. In an attempt to enhance the privacy of the President and his family, the White House installed an exterior door in the rear wall of the communications vault of the Situation Room complex that opened to a staircase going up to the swimming pool. Both the Fords and the Carters took advantage of this more unobservable route to the pool.

Sally Botsai, the deputy director under Ford, recalled what happened when President Ford cut through the Sit Room to the pool. "The President's visits were often after hours, when the Sit Room was quiet, said Botsai. "Sometimes the duty officers had only a few moments to clean up the place, shoving all the magazines, half eaten sandwiches, and trash into desk drawers, putting their shoes on, and running combs through their hair."

Amy Carter, the President's young daughter, used the back way to the pool, as did her parents, President and Mrs. Carter. Dennis Chapman, the Situation Room director under Carter, recalled a pool trip by the Carters in which Mrs. Carter was not pleased with her husband.

"She had apparently thought that no one would be present along the shortcut to the pool," said Chapman. "They came through the Sit Room and she had a robe over her swim suit and a towel wrapped around her head. She was surprised when she saw the duty officers and she gave the President the business on the way up the steps. President Carter just grinned."

By the time I arrived in the Situation Room in 1985, the NSC had made incremental improvements to the suite of rooms, including new workstations for the duty officers and analysts. During a renovation in the first Reagan term, construction crews removed the back door to the swimming pool. In 1987, we excavated part of the hill that was behind the chief-of-staff's garden and next to the pool, and constructed a room to house a new, secure video teleconferencing system. The system proved to be quite valuable during subsequent administrations during crises, but one of the initial reasons for its creation was to allow the President to confer with his advisers without public notice.

John Poindexter once asked me how we could get President Reagan's national security team into the Situation Room without the news media discovering the meeting. The press was particularly adept at noting the arrival of several limousines on West Executive Avenue, the street between the West Wing and the Old (now Eisenhower) Executive Office Building. They knew the cars meant a meeting, and if something was astir in the world, two plus two equaled a crisis meeting with the President. I figured out how to get them into the mansion without notice, but short of a tunnel under the South Lawn, they could get to the Sit Room only by walking outside along the West Colonnade to the West Wing.

In 1998, Kevin Cosgriff redecorated the conference room and the video teleconferencing room and upgraded the equipment in each so they were interchangeable. "It gave us more flexibility to have two meetings at once," said Cosgriff. "I replicated the video teleconferencing system in the front room, then refurbished the rooms one at a time, so we always have a full-up conference room in operation."

There are two entrances to the Situation Room. The front door opens off a small corridor shared with the White House Mess (so called because the Navy runs it and the traditional Navy term for an eating facility is "mess"). The other entry is through the NSC secretariat, which is located on the main hallway of the West Basement, just past the guard post manned by the Uniformed Division of the Secret Service. NSC staff members usually cut through the secretariat; visitors normally use the front door. Paul LeBras, the director from 1987 to 1989, remembers a special visitor.

"I was in the office one Saturday morning early in the Bush administration when my deputy, Ralph Sigler, stuck his head into my office and said, 'The President is at the door!' We had a miniature TV camera built into the woodwork next to the main entrance to the Situation Room to help identify visitors. Lo and behold, there was indeed George Bush at our front door."

LeBras said that Bush simply wanted to drop in and see what was going on around the world. He had picked up the phone on the wall next to the door, which automatically rang on Sit Room's secretary's desk. "This is the President. Can I come in?" he asked. Gilda Kay, the long-time Sit Room secretary, was a little flustered at first before she pushed the button that released the door lock.

"That first informal presidential visit was a far cry from the carefully scripted visits by Ronald Reagan," recalled LeBras. "We were used to unannounced Bush visits and phone calls while he was Vice President, but we were surprised when he kept some of his informal ways after his election as President."

= = =

The conference room instantly became a preferred meeting place in the White House after its construction. It was convenient to the office of the early national security advisers—Bundy and Rostow—because their desks were just steps away. (Kissinger was the first to gain the highly coveted corner office on the first floor and all of his successors, save Richard Allen, held onto it). It was then, and remains today, a small room, which Brent Scowcroft said helps keep all but principals from attending a meeting. "The Cabinet Room was too big and that table went on forever," he said. "The conference room was soundproofed, shielded, and, as opposed to the Cabinet Room, there were no windows for onlookers to assess who is meeting with whom." It has been the scene of casual meetings of staff members, home base for myriad formalized groups created and disbanded as new administrations gained office, and the site of profoundly significant presidential meetings and decisions.

There has been a general theme that has run through the structure and organization of the policy groups that have used the Situation Room for either routine or crisis meetings. Most administrations have created what were essentially Deputies groups, made up of the second in command at the major national security agencies. There have also been Principals committees, regardless of their actual title, whose members are Cabinet secretaries or agency heads. When the President joins the principals, the group essentially becomes either the full National Security Council or a variation of that statutory group. This tiered approach has been common in concept, if not in detail, to most of the presidents since Kennedy.

In 1962, Bundy established the first group to meet regularly in the Situation Room, the Standing Group, a quasi-Deputies Committee. The Undersecretary of State, the Deputy Secretary of Defense, the director of the CIA, and Bundy met periodically to consider matters that might later by tabled at a full NSC meeting with the President. They met initially on January 5, 1962, and resolved to meet weekly thereafter.

Carter had a similar hierarchical approach to committees, and, under Reagan, three levels of planning groups called the Situation Room home. The Crisis Pre-Planning Group was essentially a Deputies Committee, and the Vice President chaired meetings. The National Security Planning Group was a "principals-only" subset of the full NSC and they met regularly with Reagan. President Reagan met with the full NSC in the Cabinet Room, albeit infrequently, because the Situation Room was too small.

In the Clinton White House, interagency working groups often met in the conference room to conduct preliminary discussions about a specific national security matter—air strikes over Kosovo, for example. They "teed up" the subject for the

Deputies Committee, which comprised the deputy heads of National Security Council agencies—State, Defense, CIA, Joint Chiefs of Staff, and others as required. The deputy national security adviser to the President, Sandy Berger under Tony Lake, then Jim Steinberg during the second term, chaired the committee. If the deputies agreed on a course of action that merited further review, the Principals Committee met at the Sit Room table to tee up an issue for the President. The principals were, of course the Secretaries of State and Defense, the DCI, the Chairman of the Joint Chiefs, and so forth; Al Gore's national security adviser, Leon Fuerth, also attended. Clinton's national security adviser, first Lake, then Berger, chaired the meetings.

Encounters in the Situation Room, whether as part of deputies, principals, or NSC meetings, seem to bring out the best in people, according to Hal Saunders. After leaving the NSC staff in 1974, Saunders became the head of State's Bureau of Intelligence and Research, as well as Assistant Secretary of State for Near East and South Asia. "I attended a meeting in the Sit Room during the Carter administration—Brzezinski, Vance [Secretary of State], Brown [Secretary of Defense], and Turner [DCI] were there," said Saunders. "They profoundly disagreed with each other about intelligence community funding and organization, but they did so in a gentlemanly way. I think the aura of the Situation Room encourages people to respect each other, to be civilized in their arguments. I think people recognize the symbolism of the room."

While almost every meeting in the Situation Room focuses on a serious issue, humor is not banned. Retired Rear Admiral Mike Cramer, the intelligence officer (J2) for the Joint Chiefs of Staff in the early 1990s, recalled how President Clinton brought his sense of humor to the Situation Room. Cramer accompanied Secretary of Defense Bill Perry and Chairman John Shalikashvili to the White House to brief Clinton on developments in Bosnia. Also in the meeting were Vice President Gore, Secretary of State Warren Christopher, UN representative Madeline Albright, and national security adviser Tony Lake.

"It was on a Sunday afternoon and everyone was dressed informally. During the briefing, Secretary Christopher got hungry and asked the Mess to bring him an order of french fries," said Cramer. "When the President picked a few fries from Christopher's plate, the Secretary pulled the plate away from the President. Clinton laughed and ordered hamburgers and fries for everyone.

"My burger seemed a little dry and tasteless, but I was not about to complain about the President's burgers. After we had finished eating, Clinton started laughing and told us that we had just 'practiced virtual reality.' He explained that we had just eaten veggie burgers. To this day, I still don't know if he had set us up for a practical joke or he ate veggie burgers all the time."

═ ═ ═

Plenty of meetings have been held in the Situation Room to consider U.S. foreign policy, and the attendees are frequently the most august presidential advisers and aides. But with the exception of Johnson and Reagan, presidents haven't met there with their national security team as often as either the news media or the public might think. I found no record of Kennedy attending a Situation Room meeting, but Johnson spent days at a time there. Kissinger said that Nixon never met there, and Ford told me that he preferred the Oval Office or Cabinet Room for such meetings. Carter attended a fair number of NSC meetings in the Situation Room, but during his last-ditch attempt to free the U.S. hostages held by Iran, never left the Oval Office for the last two days of his presidency, sleeping on the couch.

Reagan met almost weekly in the Situation Room and liked to have crisis sessions there. Thirty minutes prior to an NSPG meeting, an assistant to the national security adviser laid out agenda and background folders, White House note pads, and water glasses at each seat. Interestingly, he also arranged nameplates at each position. Considering these people met almost weekly and there is a long-standing seating protocol in meetings with the President, based on cabinet seniority, I thought it was at best an unnecessary formality. This identification overkill continues today. In a photograph of President George W. Bush in the Situation Room in 2001, the very visible nameplates helped everyone get the right seat.

Exactly at the specified minute, President Reagan walked through the NSC Secretariat and into the Situation Room lobby. This was one of the rare chances for NSC clerks, secretaries, mail room jockeys, and Situation Room staff members to get face time with the President. He was unfailingly polite and greeted everyone warmly. He entered the conference room, sat down, ate a jellybean, and started the meeting. All the greeters left the lobby when the meeting started, but the Secret Service agents stayed and chatted up the Situation Room secretaries while the President was inside.

Although George H. W. Bush dropped by to chat with the duty officers or called them almost daily during crises, he often preferred to meet with his national security advisers in the family quarters. The "Gang of Eight," Bush's rump group that met during the Gulf War, convened in the Oval Office, while the deputies met in the Sit Room. During Clinton's time, he and Vice President Gore usually met with the Principals Committee in the Situation Room if that group wanted a presidential decision on military action. If the subject were other than military operations, Clinton usually met with his national security team in the Oval Office, Cabinet Room, or even the family quarters. According to Tony Lake, Clinton met upstairs because he liked to have large numbers of people at those meetings (the Small Group, which planned retaliation for the

African embassy bombings, excepted), and there was more room upstairs.

Was there more to these different approaches than just individual style?

Henry Kissinger wrote in his memoir, *White House Years*, that "Nixon was convinced that President Johnson had suffered from 'Situation Room syndrome,' meaning that he [Johnson] had succumbed to the melodramatic idea that the world could be managed in crisis from this room in the basement of the White House." Kissinger went on to say, "Nixon became the victim of his own criticism. Because of his attack on the Situation Room syndrome he and his associates were reluctant to assemble advisers there (or anywhere) at the first sign of trouble. He wanted to stay out of tactics or planning battles."

Brent Scowcroft, Kissinger's deputy toward the end of the Nixon administration, thought that Nixon's preference for remaining aloof from crisis management in the Situation Room reflected more his style than a conscious attempt to eschew Johnson's example. Alexander Haig, another deputy to Kissinger and later Nixon's chief of staff, echoed Scowcroft's theory. "He preferred to let his advisers meet without him, then study their written evaluation of a crisis and recommended actions."

During a tense time during the 1973 Yom Kippur War when the Soviets threatened unilateral action in the conflict, Nixon's national security advisers met without him in the Situation Room to consider possible U.S. reactions to the Soviet message. Haig, then in his role as chief of staff, left the meeting periodically to walk upstairs to the Oval Office to brief the President on the direction the discussions were taking.

Does a newspaper report describing a presidential meeting in the Situation Room mean the President is tending to business and taking either a real or potential crisis seriously? Or does such a meeting connote that things might be getting out of hand and the business-as-usual approach won't work?

Tony Lake, Clinton's national security adviser, believed that keeping the President out of the Situation Room was the best approach for managing public perceptions of crises. "The President meeting with his advisers in the Situation Room could suggest to the public that we had a crisis that needed managing," said Lake. "Meeting in the Cabinet Room suggests thoughtful, deliberate consideration."

On the other hand, Brent Scowcroft, adviser to both Presidents Ford and George H. W. Bush, thinks the media is intrigued with the mystique the Situation Room brings to an event. "I believe that the fact that a President meets with his team in the Situation Room adds gravity to the situation in the eyes of the news media," Scowcroft explained. "It shows that the President is seriously concerned about an issue or event." While no presidential press secretary I interviewed admitted to it, I suspect that there have been spokespeople who have intentionally highlighted a presidential visit to the Situation Room to emphasize the fact that the President is working the problem.

I am sure some presidents never thought about what message the location of their crisis meetings sent to the public. But Eleanor Clift of *Newsweek* may have stated the prevailing view of the news media. On an August 2001 National Public Radio show, Clift and other news media representatives offered a critique of President George W. Bush's month-long vacation in Texas. Clift and her colleagues acknowledged that Bush could communicate easily with his advisers wherever he was, and long presidential vacations really resonated only with the Washington press corps. But she went to say that if there were a national crisis, Bush would return to Washington and be where he needed to be—in the Situation Room.

In the aftermath of the horrific terrorist attacks on the

World Trade Center towers and the Pentagon on September 11, 2001, President Bush was traveling. Urged by Vice President Cheney to stay away from Washington because of possible continuing threats to the White House, Bush stopped at Offutt Air Force Base in Omaha, Nebraska. He quickly established a video teleconference with Cheney, his national security adviser Condoleezza Rice, and others who were in the White House. Bush also chaired a meeting of his National Security Council in the Situation Room later in the week, and his staff widely distributed a photograph of that event. Bush and his advisers met in the Situation Room daily in both the run-up to, and during, the military campaign in Afghanistan.

Meeting in the soundproofed and shielded conference room gives the President confidence that no one can eavesdrop on his conversations, but even the carefully guarded Situation Room cannot keep politicians from a time-honored Washington tradition—leaks to the news media. Robert Gates told a story about leaks and the Situation Room.

"Reagan was meeting with his group in the conference room and George Schultz, his Secretary of State, declared that he was fed up with leaks that put him in a bad light," said Gates. "Schultz then told Reagan that he wasn't going to speak during the meeting because what he said might be leaked to the press. He just folded his arms across his chest and didn't say another word during the meeting."

= = =

President Clinton nominated Tony Lake in late 1996 to be the director of Central Intelligence, but Lake withdrew from consideration in the face of opposition from the chairman of the Senate Intelligence Committee. After what he described as his "ungainly dismount" from public service, he wrote a book about potential threats to the U.S. in 2000. On the first page of his book, 6 Nightmares, Lake assesses the technological state of the Situation Room conference room as he remembers it from the mid-1990s.

The White House Situation Room, scene of so many intense meetings on the most dangerous crises facing our nation over the years, is surprisingly small. The conference table almost fills the room. One of the wooden panels on the wall can be opened to reveal a television screen and camera for video conferencing. But the Situation Room has no computer-generated maps or other twenty-first-century briefing devices.

One day in 1996 the president's national security team (I was his national security adviser) met for a discussion of chemical and biological terrorism. I found the low-tech setting symbolic of our position in addressing such new threats to our nation's security.

Why has one of the most important operations in the most important building in the world remained as this relatively low-tech facility?

First, one must put the level of technology employed in the Situation Room in context. The equipment and electronic systems the staff uses to perform its most important functions—alerting, reporting, and communications—are all high tech. The NSC staff has always acted to ensure that the "back end" of the Situation Room—communications and computer systems—is the best available. Lake's reference to the low-tech Situation Room is really directed toward the conference room and the absence of the high-tech display systems in the room.

Second, does the conference room need sophisticated display systems? If the answer is yes, then why haven't they been installed? None of the bright and experienced people who have worked on the NSC staff during the past forty years installed high-tech display systems in the conference room, suggesting that the answer to the first question is no, there is no need. But the issue is, of course, more complex than it seems.

Consider what information the President and his national

security adviser need to see during either routine or crisis. If Lyndon Johnson's obsession with the details of military strikes in Vietnam is the exception rather than the rule, and it appears to be, presidents generally don't need the type of information that is most useful when displayed in detail—the disposition of military forces. The National Military Command Center in the Pentagon has such displays and the Sit Room has had for years a video link with the NMCC that was able to display military details. After Lake left the White House, the Situation Room staff did install systems that can project images drawn from the duty officer computer workstations, including text, video, and overhead imagery.

What the President usually wrestles with in the Situation Room are political and politico-military issues, situations, and circumstances that are complex and hard to convert into bits and bytes. John Poindexter, one of Reagan's national security advisers, said it was easy to display military data. "But if the President and his advisers are confronting a terrorism crisis, what can you display?" asked Poindexter. "The data on problems that reach the President are often fuzzy."

Bud McFarlane, Poindexter's predecessor, said that officials met in the Situation Room with the President to give him counsel, not to be informed. "They came from their own sophisticated operations centers with all the needed information in their heads," said McFarlane. "Each must decide what they think about the situation and give their best advice to the President."

Brent Scowcroft, an adviser to Presidents Nixon, Ford, and George H. W. Bush, echoed McFarlane's thoughts and said that when a president meets with his advisers during a crisis, he doesn't need high tech, whiz-bang gadgets to consider the issues. "The President must concentrate on the facts and his options, not the gadgetry," Scowcroft said. "He doesn't need the flashing lights like those at the National Military Command Center or the Strategic Command."

President George H. W. Bush agreed that he did not need a "glitzy" Sit Room. "The tools were there to get the job done," he told me. "The big thing is to have rapid communications between the key players, and that works in the conference room."

During the Gulf War, there was certainly plenty of data to display. President Bush met with his senior advisers in the Oval Office or the Family Quarters, with General Colin Powell and Secretary of Defense Dick Cheney using hand-held charts and maps to brief the President. Frankly, Bush and other presidents of his generation—Nixon, Ford, Carter, and Reagan—were probably more comfortable with low-tech briefings.

Of particular relevance to this issue is the creation of the short-lived White House Crisis Management Center. In the aftermath of the attempted assassination of President Reagan, the NSC staff, John Poindexter included, moved to create the high-tech Crisis Management Center. Open for fewer than ten years, the facility in the Old Executive Office Building was full of sophisticated display, communications, and computer systems. There were several forces that might have undermined its use and hastened its demise—more on that in the next chapter—and one reason is that it wasn't needed.

For years many of the Situation Room staff, as well as officials who have met in the room, have bemoaned the lack of readily accessible maps of the right scale and detail, even if they were of the low-tech paper variety. "Maps were always a problem in the Situation Room," recalled Bill Odom, military assistant to Zbigniew Brzezinski. "There was never room to store enough maps to be self-sufficient, so the Sit Room always had to ask another agency to send over the right map."

Lake thought that insufficient money has been spent on the facility, which he believed needed a capability to electronically display maps and graphics. But he acknowledged that those on the NSC staff rarely have the time to plan and fund upgrades because of the immense demands on their time from routine business and the occasional crisis. Leon Fuerth, Al Gore's national security adviser during the entire Clinton administration, also decried the lack of sophisticated map displays and cited underfunding as an impediment. Fuerth also believes that since most of the people who use the Situation Room— senior White House officials—have not been on the cutting edge of technology themselves, they brought no pressure to upgrade the existing systems.

In addition to the exaggerated perceptions of the conference room in the entertainment industry, the news correspondents who cover the White House are unsure what the place looks like either. While reporters often walk by the windows in the operations area that look out toward the Eisenhower Executive Office Building, they never see the interior spaces. CNN's Frank Sesno said that he had never visited the Situation Room, but gave me his perceptions.

"Mythologically speaking, I guess that it's dark, secure, not terribly spacious, and in the bowels of the White House complex. I presume that secret meetings are held there, and it's the briefing room of both first and last resort. I expect that the staff aggregates information and disseminates it; I guess it is the White House's super-secret newsroom."

Even the foreign press has recognized the allure of the Situation Room. The British paper *The Guardian* wrote recently about public perceptions. "Perhaps it is the trappings of the Presidency—the Oval office, the secret service, the armoured limos and speeding motorcades, Air Force One and the White House Situation Room—which beguile. Hollywood fantasies like *Independence Day* have ensured that such symbols have international currency."

= = =

However disinterested President Clinton initially seemed to be about international affairs, his staff recognized the status of the Situation Room and the public relations value in giving White House guests tours of the facility. Neil O'Leary found the Clinton approach to Situation Room tours a dramatic shift.

"During the Bush years, we protected the Sit Room and rarely let anyone in except for official visitors," said O'Leary. "But there was a radical change when the Clintons arrived. Suddenly we had this Jacksonian democracy where everyone just walked in and out of the Sit Room. I remember giving tours to at least fifty or sixty Hollywood types and Friends of Bill in those early days."

However protective O'Leary was of the Situation Room during the first Bush administration, he did not know that a Russian spy visited his facility in the early 1990s.

In 1991, Aldrich "Rick" Ames, a CIA employee who had been spying for the Soviets since 1985, lunched with Roman Popadiuk at the White House. Popadiuk, then the deputy White House Press Secretary for NSC affairs, had met Ames when both were assigned to the U.S. embassy in Mexico City in the early 1980s, Popadiuk as a junior foreign service officer, Ames as a case officer for the CIA. Before lunch in the White House Mess, Popadiuk gave Ames a tour of the West Wing and the Situation Room.

Popadiuk, along with every other member of the U.S. government, did not know then that Ames was a Russian spy. In retrospect, it may seem like a terrible breach of security, but no one, even a spy, can learn much by walking through the Sit Room. On the other hand, Ames could have mentioned his tour to his handlers, even burnishing the facts to enhance his standing in the eyes of the KGB, the former Soviet intelligence agency. This sort of access, however brief and innocuous, could have meant a little extra in Ames's pay envelope from the KGB.

The duty officers maintained a bulletin board in the Sit Room called the Hall of Fame, which had pictures taken of them with the glitterari. Elliot Powell, the director from 1999 to 2001, recalled duty officer Tony Campanella telling him that there was a professional football player next door in the White House Mess. "Tony asked me if he could bring him in for a tour. I said yes, but only if he wasn't a Dallas Cowboy."

The player turned out to be Terry Bradshaw, a Hall of Fame quarterback who now works for Fox Sports. He sent me his recollections of the visit. "The most memorable impression of the White House Situation Room was the awesome, awesome power of the room, it demanded great respect. Physically, the room looked like a den and had an elegance about it . . . it did not look or feel like the sterile, military space it is portrayed to be in most movies."

Touring the Situation Room reached a more serious level later in the Clinton administration when federal investigators questioned Clinton about his ties with Indonesian businessman James Riady. The Lippo Group, for whom Riady worked, had donated hundreds of thousands of dollars to the Democratic Party, and Riady visited the White House several times. Riady boasted that President Clinton gave him a tour of the Situation Room in 1993, on the day federal agents stormed the Branch Davidian compound in Waco, Texas. During the subsequent investigation of Clinton fundraising activities, Clinton claimed under oath that he could not remember giving a tour for Riady.

In the last year of his second term, Bill Clinton spoofed his lame-duck status in a video he presented to the annual White House correspondent's dinner in May 2000. The video showed Clinton at a news conference with only one reporter present, preparing his wife's lunch, and riding a bike through the halls of the Eisenhower Executive Office Building. It also showed President Clinton locked in combat with General Hugh Shelton, Chairman of the Joint Chiefs of Staff, as they played a video war game in the Situation Room. P. J. Crowley, Clinton's deputy press secretary for NSC matters, later admitted to me that the film crew actually shot the scene in the Executive Dining Room of the White House Mess. "The two rooms had the same dark, wood-paneled look, so we didn't have to set the cameras in the Situation Room."

At a dinner held in Kiev to honor President Clinton, Tony Lake found himself in a room full of Ukrainian politicians and scientists. In a unique coincidence, he met the designer of the Soviet SS-9 intercontinental ballistic missile. Recalling his first meeting in the "Woodshed," in which Henry Kissinger argued with a CIA analyst about whether the SS-9 was accurate enough to attack U.S. missile silos or if the Soviet Union intended to target cities, Lake couldn't resist asking the scientist about the missile.

"First, I told him how I had met with Henry and the CIA to consider how the Soviets intended to use the SS-9," Lake said. "But the part about the woodshed was hard to get across in Russian. Then I asked him point blank, 'What were the SS-9 targets, silos or cities?' While the interpreter translated my question, the Russian started to chuckle. Then he shouted in English—'New York, Philadelphia, Washington!'"

= = =

The small, low-tech conference room in the Situation Room, bereft of the dramatic effects favored by Hollywood, nevertheless was the scene of one of the most profound meetings in the second half of the twentieth century. In that meeting in the fall of 1983, Ronald Reagan presided over the beginning of the end of the cold war and the subsequent disintegration of the Soviet Union.

Bud McFarlane, who had recently been named Reagan's

Charles D. "Chuck" Enright, left, with CIA director Dick Helms in 1969. Enright was the first duty officer assigned to the Situation Room, working a twenty-four-hour shift every third day from May 1961 until November 1962. *Sean Enright*

Lieutenant Commander Gerry McCabe, USN, at his desk in the Situation Room in 1962. McCabe was the first officer-in-charge of the Situation Room; he was an assistant to President Kennedy's naval aide, Tazewell Shepard, who had formal control of the Situation Room until Kennedy's assassination in 1963. *Joy Dell McCabe*

Commander Tazewell Shepard (left) hosted a breakfast in the Situation Room in 1962 for Jerome Wiesner (second from left), President Kennedy's science adviser; Dr. Janet Travell (center), the president's personal physician; and Captain G. G. Burkley (right), White House physician. *Robert Knudsen, White House/John Fitzgerald Kennedy Library, Boston, Mass.*

The conference room in 1962. It was likely the only room in the White House furnished with contemporary furniture at that time and looked like a suburban basement family room. *Robert Knudsen, White House/John Fitzgerald Kennedy Library, Boston, Mass.*

President Lyndon Johnson held frequent meetings in the Situation Room during the 1967 Six-Day War in the Mideast. Left to right: Clark Clifford, Ambassador Llewellyn Thompson, Honorable Nicholas Katzenbach, Secretary of State Dean Rusk, Chief of Staff Marvin Watson, Johnson, McGeorge Bundy, and National Security Adviser Walt Rostow. *Yoichi Okamoto, Lyndon Baines Johnson Library, Austin, Tex.*

Johnson was concerned about the Khe Sanh combat base in South Vietnam during the 1968 Tet Offensive. The NSC staff commissioned a model of Khe Sanh that depicted force dispositions and the surrounding terrain. From left to right, George Christain, Johnson, Bob Ginsburgh, and Walt Rostow examine the model in the Situation Room. Johnson's critics cited the model as an example of his micromanagement of the war. *Lyndon Baines Johnson Library, Austin, Tex.*

The Tet Offensive was a busy time for the Situation Room staff, shown here in the watch center adjacent to the conference room. At the far right in the rear of the room is Art McCafferty, the first director of the Situation Room. At Art's left is a window that refutes the myth that the Situation Room is an underground bunker. *Lyndon Baines Johnson Library, Austin, Tex., courtesy of Joe Shergalis*

Henry Kissinger, National Security Adviser to President Nixon, poses in the watch center of the Situation Room for *Newsweek* Magazine in 1969. The WHCA communications technician (left) and the duty officer are unidentified. *Wally McNamee*, Newsweek

Franklin McMahon painted this exterior view of the West Wing during the Nixon administration. In the center is the west exterior wall of the Situation Room; the right-most four windows correspond to those shown in the interior photographs. *Franklin McMahon, Corbis.*

President Gerald Ford apologized to Situation Room Director Jim Fazio, right, for the construction noise when the White House built the outdoor swimming pool. The Situation Room was located underneath the hedge that is in front of the West Wing in the far-right, rear corner of the photograph. Ford installed a door and stairs in the rear of the Situation Room so that he and his family could get to the pool without walking across the South Lawn. *Gerald R. Ford Library, Grand Rapids, Mich.*

President Jimmy Carter (at the head of the table) at an NSC meeting in the Situation Room. At his immediate right is National Security Adviser Zbigniew Brzezinski. Along the far side of the table, right to left, are Vice President Walter Mondale, Secretary of State Cyrus Vance, Chairman of the Joint Chiefs General George Brown, and Budget Director Bert Lance. The decor of the conference room reflects the upgrades that David McManis undertook during the Nixon administration. The wall paneling and table shown here remained until the late 1990s. *Jimmy Carter Library, Atlanta, Ga.*

Zbigniew Brzezinski judged a pumpkin-carving contest in the Situation Room during the Carter administration that Gilda Kay (then Gilda Cubbage), the Situation Room secretary, organized. The four women to Brzezinski's left are Donna Sirko (left), Michelle Mullen, Donna Moore, and Nancy Minking. *Jimmy Carter Library, Atlanta, Ga.*

After the 1981 assassination attempt on Ronald Reagan, many of his advisers gathered in the Situation Room to assess the crisis and discuss possible actions. National Security Adviser Dick Allen, left (with glasses and gray hair), recorded the deliberations; when the audiotapes were made public in 2001, they revealed some confusion in the room. Secretary of State Al Haig, center-rear with glasses, seemed unsure of the presidential succession process and later declared in the Press Theater that he was "in charge" during the Vice President's absence from Washington. *Ronald Reagan Presidential Library, Yorba Linda, Calif.*

During the hijacking of an American airliner in 1985, President Ronald Reagan joined his national security advisers in the Situation Room. Vice President George H. W. Bush and Secretary of Defense Casper Weinberger are on his right; Secretary of State George Schultz, Director of Central Intelligence William Casey, and Chief of Staff Donald Regan are on his left. The poster of Winston Churchill behind Reagan was a fixture in the conference room during the 1980s. *National Archives and the Reagan Presidential Library, Yorba Linda, Calif.*

President Reagan helps Bud McFarlane and John Poindexter celebrate their birthdays in the Situation Room in 1984. Left to right: Jondra McFarlane, McFarlane, Poindexter, Chief of Staff Jim Baker, WHCA communications technician Bill "Not the Judge" Clark, and Reagan. Bill Clark had a knack for finding photo ops during his long career in the Sit Room. *White House Photo, courtesy of John Poindexter*

Thanksgiving dinner in the Situation Room in 1986. The staff mess roasted the turkey for the Situation Room staff; Rosanne O'Hara, second from right, took it home to add the garnish. On the way back through the White House gate, the Secret Service guard dogs, which sniffed every car for explosives, found a special treat and almost got the bird. The author is at far right. *White House Photo*

FOR ALL THE FOLKS IN THE SITUATION ROOM — WITH BEST WISHES, Gary Brookins

1986 • RICHMOND TIMES • DISPATCH • Brookins

OURS

THEIRS

WHO KNOWS

SITUATION ROOM

ORLOV

ZAKHAROV

HASENFUS

BEIRUT

DANILOFF

U.N. AIDE SOVIET SPY?

"THE TIME HAS COME, MR. PRESIDENT, TO CONSIDER CREATING THE 'DEPARTMENT OF HOSTAGES, SPIES, AND SWAPS' ....."

A 1986 cartoon of the Situation Room by Gary Brookins, political cartoonist for the *Richmond Times-Dispatch*. That year, the White House was beset with repeated hostage and espionage crises; Brookins published the cartoon just a month before the Iran-Contra scandal broke. Note the folder labeled "Hasenfus" in the center. He was part of Ollie North's enterprise that was exposed in November 1986. *Gary Brookins*

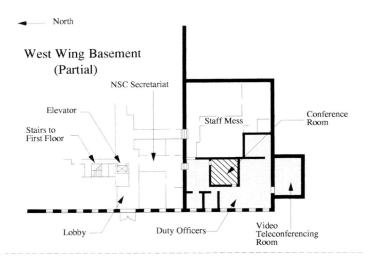

North

**West Wing Basement
(Partial)**

NSC Secretariat

Elevator

Staff Mess

Conference
Room

Stairs to
First Floor

Lobby

Duty Officers

Video
Teleconferencing
Room

West Executive Avenue

The floor plan for the Situation Room in the West Wing basement.

The conference room in 1989 remained essentially unchanged from the Ford, Carter, and Reagan years. The door at the left leads to the front door of the Situation Room complex. *George Bush Presidential Library, College Station, Tex.*

Three duty officers, along with a communications technician (not shown), man the Situation Room 24/7. This 1989 team was assigned during the Bush administration. Note that the television above the middle duty officer is tuned to CNN, as it has been since the early 1980s. *George Bush Presidential Library, College Station, Tex.*

President Clinton, center, listens to a brief in 1993 by Rear Admiral Mike Cramer, the intelligence officer for the Joint Chiefs during Clinton's first term. From left to right are Ambassador to the U.N. Madeline Albright, National Security Advisor Anthony Lake, Secretary of State Warren Christopher, Clinton, Cramer, Vice President Gore (standing), Bill Perry (partially hidden), and Chairman of the Joint Chiefs General John Shalikashvili. *White House Photo, courtesy of Mike Cramer*

President Bill Clinton and his national security team in the conference room in the late 1990s. Kevin Cosgriff, director of the Sit Room during 1997–99, refurbished the conference room and installed a new table, turning it at a right angle to the position of the old table. In the new configuration, Clinton could look directly at the TV monitors that were built in behind the paneling. The door at the rear leads to the duty officers' stations. On the far side of the table are (left to right) Director of Central Intelligence George Tenet, Chairman of the Joint Chiefs General Hugh Shelton, Secretary of Defense William Cohen, and National Security Adviser Sandy Berger. Clinton is at the head of the table with Vice President Gore to his left. *White House Photo, courtesy of Smithsonian Institution*

Tony Campanella, a duty officer from 1997–99, often took care of President Clinton's dog, Buddy, in the Situation Room. If Buddy got too rambunctious for the Oval Office, the president's stewards brought the dog down to the Sit Room until the First Family was ready for him to return upstairs. *Anthony Campanella*

President George W. Bush in the conference room with his principal advisers shortly after the terrorist attacks in September 2001. To Bush's right is Vice President Dick Cheney. To the president's left are Secretary of State Colin Powell, Secretary of Defense Donald Rumsfeld, and National Security Adviser Condoleezza Rice. The nameplates on the table have been a fixture in the conference room for years, yet seem wholly unnecessary for a group that meets so frequently. *White House Photo*

President Bush uses a video teleconferencing system at Camp David to hold meetings with his national security team, a practice that has increased since the late 1980s. *White House Photo*

The Situation Room in the television series *The West Wing*. Production designers at Warner Bros. Television used photographs from the Johnson years as guides when they created the set. They lowered the lighting and enlarged the room to enhance the dramatic effect. *Warner Bros. Television.*

third national security adviser, chaired the meeting. All of the President's principal advisers were there—Vice President Bush, Secretary of State Schultz, Secretary of Defense Weinberger, Chairman Vessey, DCI Casey, Chief of Staff Baker, Counselor Ed Meese, confidant Mike Deaver, and a few seconds on the back row. They convened to focus on the big picture of U.S.-Soviet relations.

"George Schultz started the discussion with his view that however dysfunctional Marxism may have been, the Soviet's great natural resource wealth would ensure their long life," McFarlane told me. "He suggested that we should cut the best deal possible and attempt to limit the pace of communist expansion; this was a giant we couldn't break down in our lifetime.

"'I think we can,' said someone in the back row of seats. It was Harry Rowen, who worked for Cap Weinberger," said McFarlane. "President Reagan instantly seized on his comment. 'You do?' Reagan asked him. 'Yes sir,' assured Rowen."

According to McFarlane, Rowen told Reagan that the huge Soviet bureaucracy was so inept and consumptive that despite their great resource base, the burdens on the Soviets were so immense that they were almost at a point of paralysis. Rowen suggested that if the U.S. could just impose an extra burden, the Soviet machinery would seize up.

"Cap, who was waiting to give his pitch to the President, said, 'Harry, come on . . .'" said McFarlane. "But President Reagan interrupted him and said, 'Cap, let's hear him out.'"

"To Harry's everlasting credit and without fear of his boss, Harry continued on to state that we could bring down the Soviet Union if we challenged them and made them sustain more costs," recalled McFarlane. "Later, I began to think about what we might invest in that would impose another burden on the Soviets."

McFarlane reasoned that if the U.S. invested in its strong

suit—high technology—and the Soviets responded, they would be overburdened with oppressive costs. "They were already committed to modernization of their conventional forces, so the additional costs of matching U.S. investments in strategic modernization might overload them. That meeting in the Situation Room led us to SDI [the Strategic Defense Initiative], and we spent the Soviet Union into bankruptcy."

6

CRISIS MANAGEMENT

War and Terrorism

"The President has been shot!"

Those words echoed through the halls of the White House on March 30, 1981. Just ten weeks after Ronald Reagan's inauguration, John W. Hinckley, Jr., shot the President outside the Washington Hilton hotel in Washington, D.C. Reagan was seriously wounded and the Secret Service rushed him to nearby George Washington University Hospital.

While Reagan's chief of staff, Jim Baker, and presidential counselor, Ed Meese, followed Reagan to the hospital, a gaggle of other senior advisers gathered in the Situation Room to "manage" the crisis. Richard V. Allen, the first of Reagan's six national security advisers, placed a small tape recorder on the table in the conference room and proceeded to record the group's deliberations. Allen released the tape recording in March 2001 on the twentieth anniversary of the assassination attempt, generating a good bit of news media and political interest. The reason was that the participants, the most senior national security officials in the government, seemed to be tense and ill informed. Perhaps unnerved by the potential consequences to the country if the President died, or even unsure of their roles just two months into the presidency, some of them did not sound like the kind of crisis managers the American public might want in the White House Situation Room. Showtime aired a film on cable television about the Reagan assassination attempt in December 2001 and it highlighted what a reviewer labeled "chaos" in the Situation Room. Allen criticized both the film and the characterization of the proceedings as chaotic, but writer/director Cyrus Nowrasteh defended his dramatization of the event.

During the first hour after Reagan's shooting, the group in the Situation Room was unaware of the severity of the President's wounds. They did not know if Hinckley had acted alone, or if the assassination attempt was part of a larger attack. Further, Vice President Bush was traveling, and thus unable to either immediately take temporary control of the government if Reagan were incapacitated, or to be present to succeed Reagan if the President died. Secretary of Defense Casper Weinberger wanted to increase the readiness of the Armed Forces and argued with Secretary of State and retired four-star General Alexander Haig about what actions should be taken. The two had a tense discussion about the need to have a "football" in the Situation Room, the briefcase containing nuclear weapons release codes that military personnel kept close to both the President and Vice President. One participant, Secretary of the Treasury Donald Regan, even thought about the political consequences of the assassination attempt and suggested getting out front on the right side of the handgun debate.

But the issue that got most of the news media's attention during those nervous hours in the Situation Room was the subject of presidential succession. Secretary of State Haig apparently forgot that, after the Vice President, the constitutionally mandated order of succession went through the Speaker of the House and President *Pro Tem* of the Senate before reaching the Secretary of State. Perhaps erroneously thinking that he was next in line, Haig declared, "The helm is right here."

Spokesman Larry Speakes was addressing the news media in the Press Briefing Theater upstairs and the group watched him on the Sit Room TV. When reporters asked Speakes who was running the government, he answered, "I cannot answer that question at this time." Haig rushed upstairs to breathlessly announce to the world that he was in charge.

"Constitutionally, gentlemen, you have the President, Vice President, and the Secretary of State, in that order, and should the President decide he wants to transfer the helm to the Vice President, he will do so," said Haig. "As of now, I am in control here, in the White House, pending the return of the Vice President and in close touch with him if something came up, I would check with him, of course." Haig spent a chapter in his memoir explaining what he was really trying to say.

= = =

What does *crisis management* mean? Does it mean the supervision of a threatening emergency? Perhaps in the literal sense it might, but does a president manage a crisis? Likely not, because that implies he has control over the all forces at work in a crisis. Does a president manage the country's response to a crisis? Of course. Does a president attempt to manage the consequences of a crisis? Of course. This little diversion into semantics is useful because the term *crisis management*, in the context of emergencies that both threaten U.S. citizens, property, or interests and demand presidential involvement, is overused and often misunderstood. I have to use the term *crisis management* in describing the functions of the Situation Room because most readers are familiar with these words. But I want to make it clear what crisis management at the White House is and isn't.

The Situation Room staff does not manage crises. Rather they help people who attempt to coordinate the government's response to all major international and some domestic crises. The facility provides alerting and reporting services, communications, limited surge manning, and three rooms for meetings (two in the White House, one in the Eisenhower Executive Office Building). I have to say that no one at the White House could even attempt to manage crisis consequences without all of this help from the Sit Room. Robert Gates, former DCI and deputy national security adviser to President George H. W. Bush, told me that, without the Situation Room, the White House and the NSC could never have played a role in crisis management.

The President is not involved in every crisis. Many emergencies do not merit presidential participation. Some international incidents can be monitored at a Cabinet level, and the State Department, as an example, could coordinate U.S. reaction and manage the consequences. A member of the NSC staff might join a crisis working group at State to represent the President's interests and then later brief the President's national security adviser on the highlights.

The President does not immediately go the Situation Room. If a crisis is of such magnitude that presidential involvement is needed, the President does not always "huddle with his advisers" in the White House Situation Room. The news media loves to use the hackneyed word "huddle" when describing meetings in the Situation Room. The conference room is indeed small, but it's not so cramped that men and women have to stoop over and huddle together. Maybe it's a sports meta-phor gone bad. Anyway, where the President meets with his advisers depends on his style. President Bush did meet with his advisers almost daily in the Situation Room after the terrorist attacks in September 2001, and, sure enough, one reporter said that he huddled there, another said that Bush was "hunkered down."

The cognizant NSC staff member becomes the working-level cri-sis coordinator for the White House. He or she is the point of contact for crises that reach the White House; this staffer par-ticipates in the mid-level working groups, either standing com-mittees or ad hoc groups. When a presidential decision is required, the NSC staffer will draft the decision memoranda that the President signs to initiate U.S. reaction to a crisis. The national security adviser always has a major role in White House crisis coordination.

The White House does not always take the lead in crisis coordi-nation. Reagan appointed Vice President Bush the crisis man-ager for the Executive Branch, but some cynics believed that was because Reagan's closest advisers wanted to keep Secretary of State Al Haig from that role. In other administrations, the President designated State as the lead agency for some prob-lems, Defense for others, and so on. In many instances, how-ever, the national security adviser to the President becomes the de facto coordinator, because he spends most of his noncrisis time trying to coordinate interagency actions any way.

= = =

A crisis is a crisis is a crisis is a crisis, to paraphrase Gertrude Stein. What happened, what does it mean to us, what should we do, what shall we tell the press, what are the consequences of our action are some questions common to most? Some crises seem to last forever, or they become war—the Persian Gulf War; some are over quickly—the 1983 Soviet shootdown of a Korean airliner (the consequences of that act reverberated for years, but the tension lasted only a few days). Crisis management intellectuals, such as Rich Beal during the first Reagan term, have tried to use historical analysis of past crises to development crisis management tools, but even their best intentions have been thwarted by the periodic turnover of administrations. Collective memory is easily lost at the White House, and the wheel is often reinvented every four or eight years. Some crises, those that arise gradually out of a well-reported tense situation, are more easily "managed" because every one shares a common information base before the situation becomes a crisis. Bolts from the blue—hijacked airliners ramming into New York's World Trade Center—are the toughest because it takes time to gather information and distribute it evenly amongst the crisis management participants.

To put crisis management in the Situation Room in a context, I have borrowed from a model created by Rod McDaniel, special assistant to President Reagan for Crisis Management and later NSC executive secretary. Certainly, nuances will change from president to president, but the model generally illustrates what happens in the Situation Room during a crisis.

Alerting and information gathering. What makes the bolt-from-the-blue crisis difficult to "manage" is the initial lack of information. Struggling to determine what happened is not only the first challenge, but also sometimes the hardest. The crisis session in the Situation Room on the day of Reagan's shooting was a little ragged because they didn't know the President's condition, they didn't know if other government officials were threatened, they didn't know if another country was involved, and so forth. They couldn't decide what to do until they knew exactly what happened. But they all went to the Situation Room because they knew that the duty officers would help them gather the missing information. Also, the room was centrally located and the men were used to meeting there.

When terrorists bombed the two American embassies in East Africa in 1998, the cognizant NSC staff member went straight to the Sit Room to learn more about the incidents. Richard Haass did the same when Iraq invaded Kuwait in 1990. When terrorists flew hijacked airliners into the World Trade Center and the Pentagon in September 2001, because of perceived threats to the White House, Vice President Cheney and others went to the President's Emergency Operations Center (PEOC). Cheney used that space as if it were the conference room and tried to gather more information.

Initial coordination. People immediately get on the phone to exchange information, thus begin the earliest conversations about what to do. For serious incidents that will surely involve the President, the cognizant NSC staff member will assist the deputy national security adviser in convening a Deputies Committee meeting, either in the Situation Room or via the secure video teleconferencing system that connects the Situation Room with all the other operations centers. With his deputy, Bob Gates, on vacation, Brent Scowcroft had a videoconference during the Kuwaiti invasion as did Gayle Smith during the African embassy bombings.

First on the agenda of these early meetings is an intelligence briefing from the CIA representative, then the meeting usually devolves into a discussion about U.S. actions. State is often asked to convene a working group, either ad hoc or within a standing committee, to consider U.S. options and draft an options paper. They might have only twenty-four hours to draw up the paper for consideration at another deputies meeting the next day.

During the Iraqi invasion of Kuwait in August 1990, this phase lasted for weeks. Richard Haass, the Gulf War point man on the NSC staff, literally moved into the Sit Room, taking over the office of Ralph Sigler, the deputy director.

"I camped out in the Sit Room and worked sixteen hours a day, seven days a week for three weeks," said Haass. If I wasn't meeting with the Small Group in the conference room, I was in a video teleconference with those people or others. The duty officers filtered the incoming information for me; otherwise, I would have drowned in data."

Leak prevention. McDaniel once said that if more that four people know about something, it's gone. Potential U.S. response to an incident might need to be held closely, such as when Clinton wanted to retaliate for the African embassy bombings, and interagency coordination of the draft options paper would assuredly increase the chance for leaks.

Drafting recommendations. The deputies meet in the Situation Room on Day Two to debate the options paper. Instead of distributing the paper to all the deputies before the meeting and chance a leak, State brings copies to the meeting and the first fifteen minutes of the meeting is wasted as everyone reads the paper. The objective of the meeting is to reach a consensus about U.S. actions that they can push up to the principals for consideration. Each deputy returns to his agency and briefs his principal on the pros and cons of the options and the other agencies' biases.

Briefing the President. This meeting can be in the Situation Room if that fits with the President's style, or in another White House location. Al Haig said that in the beginning of the 1973 Yom Kippur War, Kissinger, then both national security adviser and Secretary of State, wanted to meet at State. "No, Henry," Haig said, "this is the President's crisis. We will meet in the Situation Room." Although the session is usually chaired by the national security adviser, generally the DCI kicks it off with a summary of the latest information on the crisis. Then each principal voices his or her view on the situation, and the national security adviser tries to steer the group to a consensus.

Most presidents bring close advisers to these meetings who are outside of the statutory National Security Council, largely because he trusts their advice. Kennedy included Ted Sorensen and Bobby Kennedy in meetings during the Cuban Missile Crisis because he wanted their viewpoint as well as that of the generals and admirals. Since virtually everything a president does has potential domestic political ramifications, these outside advisers—Reagan brought Counselor Ed Meese and Chief of Staff Jim Baker—bring a useful perspective to situations that many think are purely in the national security arena.

Some incidents are so profound—the 2001 World Trade Center/Pentagon terrorist attack—that some of these early steps are skipped. Even though President Bush was traveling, this step in the model happened early and he met with his most senior advisers, via video teleconference, before all the deputies met and chewed over the issue.

Presidential decision. Presidents have more often than not left the meeting without making a decision. The cognizant NSC staff member will draft a presidential decision memorandum that summarizes everyone's position, and the national security adviser will take the memo to the President for a decision. The national security adviser then calls the other principals to tell them of the President's decision. George W. Bush used an approach similar to this model when he was deciding what military action to take in the aftermath of the 9-11 terrorist attacks. After his national security team presented alternatives and their recommendations, Bush withdrew, citing his need to think about the options. The next day, as the news media later reported, Bush told Condoleezza Rice, his national security adviser, of his decisions.

There have been several incidents in which the President made decisions on the spot; one involved Gerald Ford. On May 12, 1975, Cambodian gunships seized an American merchant vessel, SS *Mayaguez*, in international waters in the Gulf of Thailand. President Ford ordered U.S. military forces to speed to her assistance. While naval ships were days away, U.S. aircraft found the ship anchored near Koh Tang Island, near the coastal Cambodian city of Kompong Song. Worried that the Cambodians might try to remove the ship's crew and imprison them, Ford ordered the U.S. aircraft on scene to interdict any Cambodian ships moving from Koh Tang and the mainland, and to sink them if necessary.

During the evening of May 13 while Ford met with his advisers in the Cabinet Room, WHCA patched the Situation Room into a radiotelephone link with the aircraft orbiting over the *Mayaguez*. Also on the radio net were 7th Air Force headquarters in Thailand, the Pacific Command in Hawaii, and the National Military Command Center in the Pentagon. The aircraft reported attacking several boats, with the Cambodian gunboats returning fire. Brent Scowcroft, Ford's national security adviser, recalled what happened next. "The pilot of an Air Force A-7 told everyone that he thought he saw Caucasians on the bow of a boat headed toward the mainland. President Ford picked up his phone and the Sit Room patched him into the net. The pilot said that he had fired across the boat's bow but it continued on its course. He said that his orders were to sink the boat, but since crew members might be aboard, he was uncertain what to do next. The President told the pilot to spare

the boat." Late the next day, May 14, a Navy destroyer intercepted another Cambodian fishing boat that was carrying all
forty crewmen from the *Mayaguez*, rescuing them from Cambodian imprisonment.

Lyndon Johnson also made on-the-spot decisions during the
Six-Day War when he conducted daily Hot Line exchanges
with the Soviet Union. Because the Hot Line was activated so
frequently during the war, Johnson simply stayed in the Situation Room. In his memoir, *The Vantage Point*, Johnson described how his wife, Lady Bird, eased the stress of those
continual meetings:

> I spent many hours in the Situation Room throughout the Mid-
> dle East crisis. During some very trying days the room served
> as the headquarters of the U.S. government. On this particular
> occasion, as we sat around the conference table at dawn, Lady
> Bird brought breakfast to us. She had followed me from the Ex-
> ecutive mansion, helped prepare the food for us in the White
> House staff mess, and aided the stewards in serving it. Over
> scrambled eggs, in the crisis center of America, we reviewed the
> message from Moscow.

Joe Shergalis was on duty that morning in the Situation
Room and remembered Mrs. Johnson's arrival. "She came in
the conference room still in her robe and bed clothes. She was
upset, not because of her attire, but for bringing too little food.
She didn't know that so many people were with President
Johnson."

Follow-up. This cycle may repeat during a prolonged crisis such
as the Gulf War or the war in Afghanistan against the Taliban
and al Qaeda forces. The Situation Room maintains its alerting
and reporting functions, and the NSC staff monitors government actions to determine if the President's decision is exe-

cuted. Is that really necessary? The answer is yes—a Secretary of Defense once ignored a presidential order with which he disagreed during a crisis.

There have been so many crises since 1961 that they seem to run together. Some were over quickly; others lingered dangerously. One prolonged crisis, the Vietnam War, forced Lyndon Johnson to forego an attempt for a second term in 1968; another, the Iran hostage crisis of 1979–80, appeared to have doomed Jimmy Carter's bid for reelection.

═ ═ ═

> If I left the woman I really loved—the Great Society—in order to get involved with that bitch of a war on the other side of the world, then I would lose everything at home. All my programs. All my hopes to feed the hungry and shelter the homeless. . . . But if I left that war and let the communists take over South Vietnam, then I would be seen as a coward and my nation would be seen as an appeaser and we would both find it impossible to accomplish anything for anybody anywhere on the entire globe.

So said Lyndon Johnson, according to Doris Kearns Goodwin in her landmark biography, *Lyndon Johnson and the American Dream*. He was describing the predicament in which he found himself in early 1965. Johnson ultimately agreed to the proposal from his most senior military advisers to increase the military effort in Vietnam by bombing North Vietnam. Goodwin wrote that the Joint Chiefs of Staff predicted that large-scale, strategic bombing could destroy the industrial base of North Vietnam in about twelve days if an all-out effort were undertaken. But Johnson's political advisers suggested an incremental approach, gradually escalating the scale of bombing. Johnson agreed, fearing that China or the Soviet Union might join the conflict in response to a dramatic shift to widespread attacks. "I saw our bombs as my political resources for negotiating a peace," Johnson told Goodwin.

Johnson's use of bombs to bargain with the North Vietnamese without words led the President, Goodwin suggests, to interpose himself in the selection of targets. Johnson wanted to weigh not only the impact on North Vietnam of each strike, but also the potential unintended consequences. "What if one of those targets you picked today triggers off Russia or China?" Johnson said to Goodwin. "What happens then?"

The Situation room helped the President wage what some have called "Johnson's War." He met with military planners there to select targets. The duty officers became his personal bomb damage assessment team, gathering information from afar each night in order to answer the inevitable questions from the President, usually just before he went to sleep and again as he arose. Lyndon Johnson put a lot of pressure on those young duty officers in his unrelenting demand for information.

Johnson secretly taped many of his phone calls and some, in which he asked the Sit Room duty officer for a Vietnam update, have been saved and are catalogued in the Lyndon B. Johnson Presidential Library in Austin, Texas. The tapes give a listener a revealing insight into Sit Room operations during Johnson's presidency.

"This is the President. How are my boys doing?" The President spoke with a gravelly and rough voice, savaged not just by a few short hours of sleep, but years of whisky and cigarettes.

"Good morning Mr. President. There was a firefight south of such-and-such, and five VC were killed, at least nine wounded." The duty officer's voice wavered a bit, betraying his relative inexperience in fielding presidential hardballs at dawn.

"What else?"

"Navy aircraft attacked suspected NVA [North Vietnamese Army] trucks north of such-and-such, one plane was shot down, but the pilot is OK."

"How was he shot down?"

"I don't know, sir. We are still checking"

"What about Pat's unit? Did they see any action yesterday?" [Johnson's two sons-in-law, Pat Nugent and Chuck Robb, both served in Vietnam, and the President frequently asked about the activity of their respective units.]

"No, sir. Nothing reported."

Art McCafferty, the Situation Room director during the Johnson years, worked hard to keep his duty officers ready for these presidential queries. He gave them instructions in a 1966 memo on how to handle slow nights.

"Even though it is a quiet period and nothing unusual is occurring, it is not a good practice to start your briefing with the statement 'everything is quiet, nothing is going on,'" wrote McCafferty. "It would be good practice to remember that the person you are briefing would like to make that judgment himself. Therefore, please keep in front of you at all times a few items from the press or cables that you can talk from. It would be wise to make notes to yourself as you read the press or cable traffic on pertinent points, which you might mention."

The Sit Room duty officers wrote daily and weekly summaries of events in Vietnam for President Johnson. So did every other command center in Saigon, Hawaii, and Washington. But McCafferty soon realized that reports from State, NMCC, DIA, and others often did not provide exactly what Johnson wanted, or when. McCafferty's audience of one was hard to please, and Art's reaction was, "We'll just do it here."

Goodwin also wrote how the anxiety associated with picking the wrong target often kept Johnson from a good night's sleep, lying awake and questioning his decisions. "I would then begin to picture myself lying on the battlefield at Da Nang," Johnson told Goodwin. "I could see an American plane circling above me in the sky. I felt safe. Then I heard a long, loud shot. The plane began to fall, faster, faster, faster. I saw it hit the ground, and as soon as it burst into flames, I couldn't stand it any more.

I knew one of my boys must have been killed that night. I jumped out of bed, put on my robe, took my flashlight, and went into the Situation Room." Goodwin believed that the Situation Room was the perfect early-morning escape for Johnson. It had everything he needed at 3:00 A.M.—"people, light and talk."

The Tet Offensive of 1968 was a difficult time for Johnson, and he increased the frequency of his calls to the Situation Room. While the Viet Cong and NVA conducted scores of coordinated attacks throughout South Vietnam commencing January 31, including a brazen attack on the U.S. embassy in Saigon, Johnson zeroed in on the fighting around the Khe Sanh combat base in the northwest corner of South Vietnam.

Intelligence reports a few weeks earlier indicated that elite NVA units were massing near Khe Sanh, and an NVA defector confessed that the North wanted Khe Sanh to be another Dien Bien Phu. He said initial attacks were scheduled for early January; the main assault was planned for Tet, the lunar New Year. Dien Bien Phu was the site where the French lost the First Indochina War in 1954. Vietnamese forces surrounded ten thousand French soldiers, and the French eventually surrendered in disgrace. Dien Bien Phu was not just a location, or even the name of a battle, it was more a synonym for the defeat of a Western power in Asia. Johnson became absorbed with the potential parallel between Khe Sanh and Dien Bien Phu. Reportedly, Johnson didn't want Khe Sanh to become his "Dinbinphoo," as he pronounced it, and asked the Situation Room to update him on the status there on a near-continual basis.

The Situation Room staff arranged for the creation of a photomosaic of the Khe Sanh area, and they hung it on one of the walls in the conference room so Johnson could put reports in a geographic context. The NSC staff also commissioned a tabletop model of the Khe Sanh area so the President could understand the terrain surrounding the combat base. Publishers widely reproduced a photograph of Johnson and Walt Rostow examining the model in the Situation Room, and many writers cited Lyndon Johnson's "sand box" model as primary evidence of Johnson's micromanagement of the war. The model, which was not made of sand, rather a plaster of sorts, still exists today, gathering dust in the basement of the LBJ Library in Texas. The NVA never overran Khe Sanh; the final action there coincided with Lyndon Johnson's address to the nation in April 1968 when he announced a partial bombing cessation in the North and his decision not to run for reelection.

═ ═ ═

On January 20, 1981, just a scant ninety minutes before Ronald Reagan's inauguration as fortieth President of the United States, Gary Sick sat in the Situation Room with a telephone at each ear. One was a secure phone linking him to an intelligence center that was attempting to monitor the status of fifty-two American citizens who had been held hostage by Iran for the past 444 days. The second phone was an open line to President Jimmy Carter, who at that moment was about to walk out to the White House portico to welcome President-elect and Mrs. Reagan to their new home. Negotiations between the Carter administration and Iran had yielded, at 5:00 A.M. earlier that morning, an agreement by Iran to release the hostages. Had those hostages been released before the previous November's election, Jimmy Carter might still be President. Now, Carter was just hoping for their release before Reagan took the oath of office.

Intelligence indicated that the hostages had boarded two aircraft for their flight out of Iran, but the planes were still on the ground. Just as the motorcade bearing the Reagans and President and Mrs. Carter departed the White House for the Capitol for the inauguration ceremonies, Tehran domestic news radio reported that the hostages' release was imminent.

Sick, a naval intelligence officer serving as the point man on the NSC staff for Iran, called Carter through a phone in the limousine with that news, but also told him that intelligence sources had not confirmed the release. Sick and Carter—and much of the world—waited.

Fourteen months before, on Sunday, November 4, 1979, three thousand Iranian student demonstrators swept over the wall surrounding the U.S. embassy chancery in Tehran, trapping more than sixty Americans on the second floor. Observers thought the seizure was in response to the arrival of the Shah of Iran in the U.S. on October 22, 1979. The Shah, who had abdicated his throne in the face of an Islamic revolution earlier in the year, had left his exile in Mexico to seek medical treatment in New York.

Three Americans, including the embassy charge d'affaires, Bruce Laingen, were at the Iranian Foreign Ministry at the time of the seizure and remained there as hostages until they joined the rest in January 1981. Fourteen of the original hostages were released early, leaving fifty-two in prolonged captivity.

On the day following the hostage taking, Zbigniew Brzezinski, President Carter's national security adviser, chaired a meeting of the Special Coordination Committee (SCC) in the Situation Room. The group consisted of Carter's senior national security advisers; it met almost daily for long periods over the coming year to consider developments and to plan U.S. actions.

In preparation for those daily committee meetings, Gary Sick arrived at the Situation Room at about 5:00 each morning to evaluate a thick file of reports and cables the duty officers had accumulated overnight. He prepared an agenda for the SCC that usually met at 9:00 A.M. in the Situation Room. Then Sick turned his notes of the meeting into a memo for the President, complete with YES and NO check boxes for action items, which Brzezinski gave to Carter each day about 11:00 A.M. "This process went on for months at a time," recalled Sick twenty-two years later. "The crisis consumed the Carter presidency and placed extraordinary demands on the Sit Room staff. Their support was critical to me and I had nothing but praise for them."

Negotiations with Iran for the release of the hostages dragged on for months. The government explored every angle, through both the secular Iranian government that followed the revolution, and the extremist Islamic clerics that had enormous influence over the hostage's captors. When those negotiations seemed to be at a dead end in April 1980, President Carter authorized a military attempt to rescue the hostages. Planning for the mission had been extremely close-held; not even the Situation Room staff knew of the pending operation.

"We knew something was up," recalled Dennis Chapman, the Situation Room director during the Carter administration. "One of my duty officers, who was good at picking up hints, offered coffee to the people in the rescue planning meetings in the conference room. When he took in the coffee and cups, he glanced at the maps in an attempt to figure out what they were doing. But when Charlie Beckwith showed up in the Situation Room in his fatigues and jump boots for a 9:00 P.M. meeting with the President, we were sure something was about to happen."

Beckwith was a highly regarded Army officer who led the Delta Force commandos on the rescue attempt. A series of tragic errors plagued the mission and Beckwith, after gaining concurrence from the Secretary of Defense and President Carter, aborted the operation when the rescue helicopters and fixed-wing support aircraft met trouble at Desert One, the secret rendezvous point in the Iranian hinterland.

"By then, the duty officers were in the loop and they called to tell me that the rescue attempt failed," said Chapman. "I

said, 'What rescue attempt?' The duty officer said, 'You know
the one we thought was going to happen? Well, it did and it
didn't work.'"

"I found out the next day that the plan called for the Situation Room to become the command center for the mission had
the hostages been extricated from the embassy," Chapman
continued. "We would have been hard-pressed to do everything the plan called for without any advance notice."

Through the presidential election campaign of 1980, President Carter worked tirelessly to gain the hostages' release. In
his 1991 book *October Surprise*, Gary Sick asserts that Reagan
confidants secretly arranged for the Iranians to hold the hostages until after the election, thus depriving Carter of the momentum he needed to surge ahead of Reagan late in the
campaign. But even after his defeat, Carter continued pressing
for an agreement with Iran that would free the hostages.

Negotiations with the Iranians, through the good offices of
the Algerian government, continued through the last few days
of the Carter presidency. Part of the final agreement with Iran
to release the hostages was the return of Iranian funds, frozen
in the U.S. after the embassy seizure. Once the final transfer
of the money to Iran was complete early on January 20, Carter
and his advisers gathered in the Oval Office to wait for news
that the Americans had boarded aircraft to leave Tehran. The
Situation Room patched the President into a secure conference call between the Sit Room and intelligence agencies monitoring the situation. The President sat quietly, listening to
periodic updates on the status of the aircraft. About 10:00 A.M.,
Carter and everyone else had to leave the Oval Office so the
White House staff could rearrange the room for Reagan. Gary
Sick and Hamilton Jordan, Carter's chief of staff for most of
the previous four years, moved downstairs to the Situation
Room where Sick proceeded to work two phone lines at a time.

Dennis Chapman remembers those last moments before

Reagan's noon inauguration. "We got word that the aircraft had started their engines, then they taxied to the end of the runway," said Chapman. "We relayed that info to Phil Wise, Carter's personal assistant, as the motorcade approached the Capitol, but then we heard that the aircraft had turned off their engines. Then about ten minutes to twelve, Ham Jordan just went nuts. He turned to me and said, 'They aren't going to let them go while Carter's still the President. They won't give him that satisfaction.'"

Earlier that morning, Zbigniew Brzezinski asked Chapman to brief Jim Brady and Dick Allen on the hostages' status. Brady would become Reagan's press secretary and Allen his national security adviser, and both were at the Blair House across the street from the White House. "He said to just give them what was in the press, nothing classified," Chapman recalled. While Chapman did not offer an opinion why Brzezinski withheld the latest intelligence reports from Reagan's staff, one might infer that Brzezinski was as frustrated as Jordan was about the apparent Iranian manipulation of the exact time of the release of the hostages.

The planes carrying the hostages to freedom departed Tehran's airport after Reagan's swearing-in and while former President Carter was en route by helicopter to Andrews Air Force Base. The crisis, which not only consumed the last year of the Carter presidency but also probably doomed it, came to a merciful end, albeit too late for Jimmy Carter.

= = =

The Situation Room flap in the aftermath of the attempted assassination of Ronald Reagan led to the creation of an adjunct to the Situation Room called the Crisis Management Center. John Poindexter, President Reagan's fourth national security adviser, recalled the circumstances.

"There was a good bit of consternation among the President's most senior advisers—Baker, Meese, and Deaver—

about the functioning of the Situation Room following the shooting of the President," Poindexter said. "They wanted a study undertaken to examine the Sit Room's concept of operations and compare that with what it should be. The White House asked me to become Dick Allen's military assistant and, after reporting to the White House in June 1981, I spent most of that year reviewing the history of the Sit Room, as well as what happened during the assassination attempt."

Poindexter said that he found that the Situation Room performed just as it had been designed. While its technological shortcomings were evident, Poindexter determined that the problem lay in the difference between what the Sit Room had always been and what Reagan advisers thought it was. "They thought it was a decision or command center set up to facilitate high-level decision making," explained Poindexter. "It was really more of a switching center where duty officers routed incoming information to the NSC staff, the national security adviser, and other White House officials."

Poindexter then embarked on a three-phase upgrade to the crisis management capabilities at the White House. First, create a true, technologically advanced crisis management facility along the lines of what Reagan's staff envisioned. Second, upgrade the information technology in the Situation Room. And last, install a secure, closed-circuit television system that linked the White House with the other national security agencies— State, the Pentagon, CIA, and others.

Poindexter enlisted the help of an assistant to Ed Meese, Dr. Richard S. Beal, to conceptualize a crisis management center, then build it. "We needed to supplement the Situation Room and create a place that could take over a crisis while the Sit Room continued to watch the rest of the world," recalled Poindexter. "We wanted a room big enough to install large-screen displays and accommodate large, interagency meetings. The Sit Room could not be expanded—the swimming pool, the staff mess, and the street outside restricted it. Also, the staff was too small to analyze crisis information or plan for future crises."

Poindexter and Beal, who became senior director for crisis management systems and planning, hit on the idea of converting Room 208 in the Old Executive Office Building across the street from the White House. After extensive reconstruction of the room and surrounding spaces, the Crisis Management Center, or CMC, opened in 1983; a staff separate from the Situation Room manned the facility. They worked normal hours during noncrisis times, but manned up 24/7 to support what Poindexter called "crisis consequence management." He convinced the Department of Defense to pay for the new center. "Frank Carlucci, then at the Pentagon, was not easily swayed," Poindexter said. "He told me to just call the Pentagon whenever the White House needed data, but he finally, grudgingly, acquiesced and approved the funding."

"Our objective was to organize and display information relevant to the crisis in an interactive and adaptive way," continued Poindexter. "It was difficult then because the underlying technology either didn't exist then or it was just in its infancy. While fiber optic local area networks (LANs) are commonplace today, we struggled to find those systems in 1983 to connect the CMC to the Situation Room. There were no PCs then to use as terminals or workstations; the most advance piece of equipment in the Sit Room then was a magnetic card typewriter."

The conference room in the new CMC had been the Secretary of State's old office where, on December 7, 1941, Secretary of State Cordell Hull received the Japanese Ambassador just before the attack on Pearl Harbor. The period grandeur of the room had been retained, complete with murals and artwork on the plaster walls. Behind discrete paneling were the large screen displays for the projection of maps, charts, intelligence reports, and drafts of outgoing cables.

First, the staff installed seven powerful VAX computers adjacent to the conference room. Second, terminals to those computers were installed in the Situation Room, and they were used also to satisfy Poindexter's other goal of upgrading the information-processing capabilities there. Third, technicians installed a secure video teleconferencing network in operations centers throughout Washington. The White House had two of the terminals, one in the CMC and the second in a room in the back of the Situation Room.

The NSC staff first used the CMC for interagency planning for the U.S. invasion of the Caribbean nation of Grenada in 1983. However, the NSC staff made limited use of the CMC throughout the Reagan administration, mainly because it lost its most ardent disciples. Rich Beal died unexpectedly in 1984, and John Poindexter became the deputy to National Security Adviser Bud McFarlane in 1983. Beal was the resident intellectual and the guiding light for the CMC, the person who tried to use technology to help synthesize information for decision makers. Without his vision, the operational concept of the CMC became clouded. Poindexter, who later succeeded McFarlane as Reagan's national security adviser in 1985, became too busy to guide the CMC toward the objectives that he and Beal had sought. In 1986, Poindexter resigned his position in the face of the gathering storm known as the Iran-Contra scandal.

David Aaron, deputy to President Carter's national security adviser, Zbigniew Brzezinski, wrote a novel published in 1987, *State Scarlet*, just about the time Room 208 became tainted by connections to Oliver North's Contra support operation. Aaron, much to Dick Allen's chagrin and public consternation, referred to the room in his book as "Allen's Folly" because of Allen's role in conceiving the CMC and its relative lack of success. In fairness to Dick Allen, Judge Bill Clark had replaced Allen and become Reagan's second national security adviser long before the CMC opened its doors.

By the late 1980s, the CMC had almost withered away. The NSC broke up the staff and the individuals became analysts for the Situation Room. They were assigned to help the major geographic and functional NSC staff elements, but personnel cutbacks eventually eliminated those positions. At the beginning of President George H. W. Bush's administration in 1989, the CMC existed in name only. Bush's national security adviser, Brent Scowcroft, did not see the need to use it at all. "I closed it down," Scowcroft said.

Scowcroft's boss, former President Bush, told me that the small conference room in the Situation Room was all he needed. "The facilities were cramped, but I think it was important that the Situation Room be located in the White House itself, not in the Old Executive Office Building."

7

REPORTING

"Good Morning, Mr. President"

"I have a report for President Kennedy," Commander Gerry McCabe told the President's valet.

"Yes sir, he is expecting you. He's in the bathtub, but go right in."

"Bathtub," gasped McCabe. "Don't you think I should just leave it with you?"

Just then, Kennedy yelled from inside with his distinctive Boston accent, "Come on in, Commander."

McCabe's widow, Joy Dell, told that story, describing how embarrassed her late husband was when, as the first officer in charge of the Situation Room, he delivered a report to the presidential bathroom during the Cuban Missile Crisis in 1962. "Gerry told me that he waited until Kennedy read the report then, not knowing what else to do, saluted the President and left," said Mrs. McCabe.

The Situation Room staff has been writing reports for the President and the White House staff since 1961. In addition to their alerting, communications, and crisis support responsibilities, the duty officers have written both daily summaries of world events and spot reports describing developments that can't wait for the next summary. Some presidents demanded great detail; others, just the highlights. The early reports were written out by hand and hurriedly typed by secretaries trying to meet a deadline. Today, if the President is traveling, a duty officer can write a report, then the NSC representative with the President can access the report as a shared file on a remote terminal.

For those international events that are significant, yet do not meet criteria for alerting or spot reports, the duty officers and analysts have included a brief description in their daily summaries. Initially, they distributed the summary in the morning, then as interest increased, added an evening summary. The staff culled potential summary items from cables, intelligence and military reports, and news stories. When the duty officers knew that either the President or his national security adviser would be anticipating an update of a certain development, they aggressively sought out information for the next summary; in doing so, they often rankled officials outside the White House.

With Lyndon Johnson calling them every morning for news from Vietnam, the duty officers phoned the headquarters of the U.S. Military Assistance Command, Vietnam (MAC-V) headquarters in Saigon. During the Tet Offensive by the Communist forces in Vietnam in early 1968, Art McCafferty got out ahead of military protocol as the first reports of the Tet attacks began to reach the Situation Room. At 5:30 A.M. January 31 (Washington time), McCafferty knew that Johnson would soon be calling the Sit Room for a report on what had happened since his last call the night before. McCafferty was on the secure phone with MAC-V headquarters to get the latest news when Johnson indeed called the duty officer, who had to say the words dreaded throughout the Sit Room—"We have nothing new, Mr. President."

Hoping to be spared more of the President's anger, McCafferty later talked with General William Westmoreland, commander of MAC-V, then passed an update to the President. General Earle Wheeler, Chairman of the Joint Chiefs, lit into Walt Rostow later that day for allowing the Situation Room to interfere with his field commanders during the heat of battle.

In 1996 when hostile fire brought down Air Force Captain Scott O'Grady's plane over Bosnia, Situation Room duty officers got ahead of the Pentagon's reporting of the rescue of the downed pilot. "The Situation Room got updates from the intelligence community faster than the reporting from the military," said Tony Lake, Clinton's national security adviser at the time. "When I talked with Bill Owens, the vice chairman of the Joint Chiefs, I often had more recent information than he had received. That was partly because the commands in the field withheld information until they were sure it was accurate, but Owens was still upset."

The Situation Room staff has not only been aggressive in seeking out information, but also has been very good at writing their reports. The duty officers and analysts became skilled over the years in identifying important incoming information and reducing large volumes of data down to concise, synthesized reports. Cabinet-level officials recognized that skill on at least two incidents when they asked to be put on distribution for Sit Room reporting.

During the Six-Day War, President Johnson met daily in the Situation Room with his senior advisers. Johnson's national security adviser, Walt Rostow, distributed Sit Room summaries, spot reports, and selected cables on the war to everyone in the conference room. The Sit Room's product so impressed Secretary of Defense Robert McNamara that he asked Rostow to send Sit Room reporting to his office in the Pentagon. The fact that the Pentagon had many more people doing the same things as the Sit Room spoke highly of McNamara's regard for the Sit Room's reporting. While Rostow chose to ignore the request, Art McCafferty, the Sit Room director, later wrote to his staff, commending them for their efforts during the war. "I think the fact Secretary McNamara requested that we screen and transmit materials to his office in order that he could be kept informed is indicative of how well you have been able to perform your main task of keeping the President informed."

Years later, during the Carter administration, Dennis Chapman, the director of the Situation Room, briefed Zbigniew Brzezinski, Vice President Walter Mondale, DCI Stan Turner, and others on the Chinese invasion of Vietnam. "I thought I had given a thorough briefing," recalled Chapman, "and Turner confirmed that when he followed me out of the conference room. He leaned toward me and asked in a low voice, 'Can you send me copies of the reports you give to Zbig?' I took that as a huge compliment for the Sit Room, considering the vast resources available to the DCI, but I asked him to take that up with Dr. Brzezinski."

The Situation Room has also facilitated the flow of routine and crisis reporting from other agencies into the White House, most often assembling various reports into folders or reading books for the President and his staff. The duty officers don't screen those reports, but rather bundle them into coherent packages. The most significant of these reports from other agencies are the President's Daily Brief (PDB) from CIA and summaries from the State and Defense Departments. The State and Defense Departments have also forwarded regular summaries to the President, often via the Situation Room. DIA has also sent reports; however, during some administrations, those summaries were forwarded through either CIA or the Secretary of Defense.

= = =

When Kennedy took office, there was, of course, no Situation Room, so all the current event reporting came from other agencies. Following the practice of Eisenhower, who received his daily intelligence briefing from Brigadier General Andy Goodpaster, Major General Ted Clifton acted as the intelligence point man for Kennedy. He quickly grasped the new President's preference for reading rather than listening to oral briefings and for receiving the source documents, not just the summary items. The number of papers that Clifton brought into the Oval Office each day began to increase rapidly.

Clifton drew his daily intelligence briefing from the CIA daily summary, the Central Intelligence Bulletin or CIB, two summaries from State, a DIA summary, plus summaries from each military service. But in February 1961, according to a 1968 interview, Ted Clifton said that Kennedy indicated that he was receiving too much information. Clifton, Mac Bundy, and Bromley Smith helped CIA create a format that included headlines and short blurbs on events, each with a box that Kennedy could check if he wanted more information. The term *checklist* for the President's daily summary came from this format. CIA prepared the checklist every morning and, according to Clifton, Kennedy read it enthusiastically and often discussed its contents with the Secretaries of State and Defense. When Rusk and McNamara found themselves unprepared because they were unaware of an item in the checklist, CIA added them to the distribution.

Bundy and Smith forwarded nonintelligence information to Kennedy in a stream parallel to Clifton's. In a remarkably frank memo to the President in May 1961, Bundy lectured Kennedy about making time for a daily briefing. "You should set aside a real and regular time each day for national security discussion and action. This is not just a matter of intelligence briefing— though that is important and currently *not* well done by either Clifton or me (we can't get you to sit still, and we are not really professionals)."

Bundy continued his scolding. "Truman and Eisenhower did

their daily dozen in foreign affairs the first thing in the morning, and a couple of weeks ago you asked me to begin to meet with you on this basis. I have succeeded in catching you on three mornings, for a total of about eight minutes, and I conclude that this is not really how you would like to begin the day. . . . Will you try it? Perhaps the best place for it would be the new Situation Room which we have just set up in the basement of the West Wing. . . ."

In the months that followed Bundy's candid memo, the Situation Room staff began to write a daily summary of overnight events. I have included one of those reports from early 1963, remarkable only because it is one of the few unclassified Sit Room summaries in the JFK Library.

2 April 1963
Situation Room

Mr. President:
    Overnight items of interest:

Argentina: Anti-government generals proclaimed an anti-Communist revolt today. Navy reported supporting the rebels, and other armed forces alerted. The proclamation claimed the coup aimed to reestablish justice and peace, let the people work, and postpone a general election. Buenos Aires is calm.

Moscow: TASS has reported the death of Soviet Deputy Foreign Minister Georgi Pushkin, age fifty-four, apparently of natural causes.

Laos: Foreign Minister Quinim Pholsena was assassinated last night.

When Johnson became President he cancelled the daily briefings, but welcomed written reports—a number of them, in fact. CIA created the first PDB for Johnson on December 1,

1964. Initially, Johnson read the PDB in the morning, but then ignored the report for a period of time. Later he asked for the daily CIA report in the evening, and his secretary included it in what was called Johnson's "Night Reading." In the fall of 1965, Bromley Smith created the following list of the reports that either the Situation Room or Mac Bundy sent to President Johnson.

7:00 A.M.	Daily. Situation Room summary of crises (Vietnam, India-Pakistan, Dominican Republic), drawn from information from NMCC, CIA and State.
8:30 A.M. to 9:00 P.M.	Daily, except Sunday. Spot reports, typed cables from the field, action and information memoranda.
7:00 P.M.	Monday–Friday (2:00 P.M. Saturday). President's CIA Intelligence Brief.
7:30 P.M. to 8:00 P.M.	Monday–Friday. USIA [U.S. Information Agency] Foreign Press Reaction Report.
7:30 P.M. to 8:00 P.M.	Monday–Friday. State Department Evening Report to the President.
10:45 P.M.	Daily. Situation Room summary of latest developments, primarily military (comparable to the morning report).

Reporting on the Vietnam War got the most attention in the Situation Room. Below are fragments from a memo that a duty officer sent Johnson on November 2, 1965, and it is representative of the kind of detailed reports that Johnson wanted. (The Johnson Library declassified the summary.)

MEMORANDUM FOR THE PRESIDENT

SUBJECT: Military Situation in South Vietnam for the Week
24–30 October 1965

1. The pace of the war quickened for the third week in a row
with the Viet Cong attacking in regimental strength in. . . .
2. The first round in the battle for Plei Me ended October 27
when an estimated two Viet Cong regiments broke contact
under pressure from. . . .
3. In Phu Yen Province, where South Vietnamese units are attempting to provide security for the rice harvest, friendly
forces inflicted heavy casualties on the enemy in three
engagements. . . .
4. On October 27, an estimated two Viet Cong battalions
launched an attack. . . .
5. Statistically, total Viet Cong incidents dropped to 782 from
811, representing a decline in anti-aircraft fire and propa-
ganda incidents. The number of Viet Cong attacks increased
to fourteen from nine, terror incidents to 446 from 444, sab-
otage incidents to 105 from ninety-nine.

Casualties for the week 24–30 October

	Killed	Wounded	Missing/Captured
Viet Cong	1,264		133
South Vietnamese	364	774	63
U.S.	23	114	2

"President Johnson was a demanding consumer," said Joe
Shergalis, one of his duty officers. "Sometimes he stood next
to our desk, all 6'4" of him, and asked us what was going on.
He was an intimidating figure and he never joked about anything."

John Helgerson wrote about the PDB history in a paper published by CIA's Center for the Study of Intelligence in 1996.
Helgerson reported that Johnson returned to reading the PDB

in the morning late in his presidency, and a White House photo provided evidence of that habit. In the photo, Johnson and his wife had their bedclothes on and Mrs. Johnson was holding their young grandchild; Johnson held the PDB with its title page clearly visible.

Before he became the Situation Room director in 1969, David McManis, an Arab linguist and analyst, served as the liaison between NSA and the Situation Room during the period 1966 to 1969. McManis traveled almost daily from NSA headquarters at Fort Meade, Maryland, near the Baltimore-Washington Airport to the White House to help Situation Room duty officers make the best of the huge amount of signals intelligence that NSA produced. It was in that position in August 1968 that McManis saw a number of anomalies in Warsaw Pact and Soviet military forces near Czechoslovakia. During the preceding months, the Soviet leadership had become uncomfortable with growing liberalism in the Czech communist government. What McManis saw in the intelligence reporting were indications that the Soviet Army, along with token military support from their East European satellites, might be preparing to invade Czechoslovakia.

"I pulled together a note for Walt Rostow, President Johnson's national security adviser, that described the situation and why I thought something was up," recalled McManis. (Later in his career, McManis became the national intelligence officer for warning.) "Rostow, who had perfected the art of writing concise memos, had me turn my note into a one-page memo to the President. Although the DCI, Richard Helms, sent down a similar warning to Johnson, it was about twenty-four hours after I wrote mine."

According to McManis, the President is well served by having the Sit Room sort through warning information independently from the major suppliers of national security information. More than thirty years later, McManis recalled:

The Czech invasion highlighted the institutional biases of the agencies. CIA's emphasis on human intelligence [reporting from foreign agents and sources] often colored their reporting. Observations by embassy personnel drove State's reporting, and military attaches in those same embassies influenced DIA's reporting. NSA, of course, produced nothing but signals intelligence [intercepts of communications and electronic systems such as radar]. While the DCI should have had access to everything, the Situation Room often had to attempt to, on their own, synthesize data from disparate sources for the President.

The North Korean shootdown of an U.S. Navy reconnaissance aircraft in April 1968 provided another example of ill-coordinated, downright messy reporting of events by the various agencies. The EC-121 aircraft was a forerunner to the Navy EP-3 aircraft that barely landed in China after a collision with a Chinese fighter jet in 2001. McManis recalled the confusion surrounding the event:

> While Defense Department concentrated on finding survivors, attention at the White House turned to the location of the plane when the Chinese attacked. Was it in international waters, or had it penetrated North Korean airspace? Every agency sent its own chart with the aircraft's track and location. CIA's was too general, DIA's was flat wrong, and none of them matched up with each other. NSA had the most accurate data, but I had to drive out to Fort Meade to get everything plotted on one chart. It took me eight hours to get a chart that was accurate enough to show the President.

These poorly coordinated flaps have over the years frustrated the Situation Room staff in their attempt to rapidly write a coherent report on fast-breaking events. That frustration has produced an attitude that says, "We'll just do it here!" Besides, when the President calls the duty officer for an update, as Johnson did daily, the duty officer has to answer the mail, not explain that CIA sent the wrong map.

= = =

When the presidency changed hands in 1969, Situation Room reporting changed with it. Al Haig, then an assistant to Henry Kissinger, and David McManis, the new director of the Situation Room, began to develop the process of assembling a daily package for Nixon. McManis recalled:

> I gathered together at the end of the day those items that I thought the President should see. Some were short summaries that I had written and the NSC staff submitted others. We also drew items from the intelligence agencies and State. We drafted a two- or three-page summary that I gave to Haig in the evening to review. At first Haig wanted me to bring him the draft and wait for comments. This often lasted until 11:00 P.M., and since I had been in the Situation Room since 6:00 A.M. that day, I started just leaving the draft for him to annotate.

McManis made any changes that Haig had requested the next morning, then added any significant overnight developments. "We put our summary in a folder with State's summary and the PDB and sent it up to Kissinger," said McManis. "Richard Helms, the DCI, tried to interest Nixon in oral briefings, but the President preferred reading the PDB."

An analyst in the Situation Room from 1972 to 1974, Sally Botsai helped McManis prepare the morning summary. "I arrived at 5:00 A.M. and started with the draft from the previous night that our secretary had typed on a magnetic tape typewriter," Botsai said. "The MAC-V report, which summarized all the military events in the last twenty-four hours in Vietnam, Laos, and Cambodia and had to be in our summary, arrived between 5:30 and 6:00 A.M." Botsai had to condense the report, check it for accuracy, and get it to the secretary for typing as soon as possible. Since Kissinger wanted it to be the first item in the Sit Room summary, none of the other items could be finished until the secretary typed the MAC-V highlight. "Murphy's Law often meant that something always delayed the report, and the secretary and I were in low orbit by 7:30 A.M. trying to get the summary to Kissinger before 8:00. Mondays were particularly chaotic since our secretary, Maryellen Abell, drove from her beach house straight to work."

The Situation Room's woes about disconnected reporting from outside agencies continued during the 1973 Yom Kippur War. Sally Botsai remembered the trouble she had responding to detailed questions from Kissinger. "The folks upstairs were interested in the number of Soviet air transports going into the UAR, and their cargo became a focus of great attention," said Botsai. "But the community reported widely differing numbers and we took a lot of abuse for the discrepancies in the reports. After many phone calls around the community, we discovered that each report used a different cutoff time, making it all but impossible to get an accurate count. After speaking with the head of DIA, Lieutenant General Danny Graham, DIA assured me that they would be able to reconcile the numbers, and the complaints from upstairs diminished."

When Gerald Ford became President after Nixon's resignation, CIA briefers delivered the PDB directly to Ford. According to John Helgerson, that routine lasted only until November 1975 when Brent Scowcroft, Ford's national security adviser, began bringing the PDB to Ford with other briefing materials.

= = =

"Good morning, Mr. President," said Dennis Chapman as he stood next to Jimmy Carter in the Oval Office.

"Just a minute, Dennis, I'll be right with you," Carter said as he read the morning paper.

Chapman found himself that January morning in 1981 on

unfamiliar ground. As the director of the Situation Room throughout the Carter administration, he normally came in early to sort through the materials the duty officers had collected overnight that might merit presidential attention. He then filled a folder with the Situation Room Morning Summary, the PDB, parts of the State Department Summary, and some individual cables and intelligence reports. Chapman then gave the folder to Zbigniew Brzezinski, Carter's national security adviser, who, according to Chapman, "tore out parts, added other information, and stapled everything together for the President." Brzezinski gave the folder to Carter at their regular morning national security meeting.

One morning just a few days before Carter left office, Brzezinski couldn't get into the White House on time and called Chapman. "He asked me to gather up the morning 'take' and deliver the folder to the President," said Chapman. When the Secret Service called the Sit Room to notify them that "POTUS" (President of the United States) had left the residence for the Oval Office, Chapman nervously walked upstairs. He said that he had never accompanied Brzezinski to his morning session with Carter and had no idea what the routine was during that meeting:

> I explained to Susan Clough, the President's secretary, about Dr. Brzezinski's problem and that I was standing in for him. She said, "Go right in," and opened the door to the Oval Office. "Dennis Chapman from the Sit Room is here to see you, Mr. President. Dr. Brzezinski is late again," apparently referring to a running joke between her and Carter about Brzezinski's habits.
>
> As I entered the Oval I saw that the President was sitting by the fire at the end of the room opposite from his desk. He was reading the stock quotes in the newspaper with his back to me. It was just me, the President, and nobody else, and my mind

started racing with what could go wrong. If I approached him from the right, he might turn and bump into the lamp next to him. If I went to the left, I might trip on the edge of the rug. Fortunately, neither happened and he graciously accepted the folder and read it quietly while I waited.

Chapman said that the informal folder that he and Brzezinski prepared for Carter did not appeal to Dick Allen, President Reagan's first national security adviser. "Allen asked me to find a leather folder in a color that the President would like and have it embossed with the presidential seal."

= = =

Situation Room reporting under Reagan took a slightly different turn from the Carter practices, a change that is common whenever a new president takes office.

For most of Reagan's eight years, the Situation Room filled his dark-red leather folder with several reports, rarely changing the mixture because the President prized a set routine. The folder displayed the PDB, a five- or six-page, full-color pamphlet, prominently on the right side. CIA sent down an advance copy by secure fax early in the morning so that the duty officers and the analyst could eliminate duplicate items in other reports for the President. Couriers brought the hard copy from CIA about 6:00 A.M.

A courier from State brought their daily summary, which the analyst tucked behind a leather tab on the left side of the President's folder. The analyst also included a daily memo to the President from the Situation Room in which the staff summarized two or three issues that fell below the threshold of the PDB. The Situation Room "day workers" wrote the items the previous day, after I met with them to discuss potential subjects. CIA routinely sent down executive summaries of National Intelligence Estimates for the President, but the five to ten pages were too long for Reagan. We reduced them to two paragraphs and included the miniversions in our daily memo.

Fred Wergeles, an analyst from CIA approached me one day with a copy of a major study he had authored at CIA about Soviet air defenses before coming to the White House. He jokingly suggested that his work truly merited a review by Reagan. Fred reminded me of the incident years later. "You told me to go ahead and write it up for the President, but you said no more than five sentences," Wergeles recalled. "I reduced three or four years of work into five lines, but when the memo came back the next day with "RR" in the corner, I was elated."

Defense sent over a weekly summary on Saturday morning and the duty officer placed that in the leather folder. I never understood why they defaulted the daily reporting to CIA and State. CIA also included a weekly military intelligence report from DIA in the Saturday PDB.

Every weekday morning, duty officers gave the completed President's folder to a military driver, who picked up the national security adviser at home and drove him to the White House. Bud McFarlane or his successors while I was in the Situation Room—John Poindexter and Frank Carlucci—reviewed the folder's contents during the ride into the office, occasionally asking that we make last-minute changes. The Sit Room analyst would make those changes while McFarlane chaired the daily NSC staff meeting in the Sit Room conference room. After the staff meeting, the national security adviser added papers to the folder that he had set aside for the President, then carried the folder into his daily meeting with Reagan.

At the specific request of the national security adviser, we made photocopies of the PDB for limited distribution to senior White House staff members. DCI Bill Casey heard about the practice and was displeased. Bob Gates, who was then the deputy director of CIA for intelligence, told me later that CIA stopped including the most sensitive items in the PDB because of this extracurricular distribution.

The duty officers collected material for the twice-daily Situation Room summaries throughout the day and night, even writing first drafts of items as they went along. We had two analysts alternating the day and night shifts. The night analyst arrived about midnight and drafted/edited the morning summary. The day analyst did the same for the evening summary. We distributed the summary to just about everyone from the Vice President on down.

I changed the long-standing format of the Situation Room summary in 1985 after I happened to read a copy of the *Kiplinger Washington Newsletter*. Austin Kiplinger published a series of newsletters, and his staff used a distinct style that his readers, many of whom were business executives, found easy to read. I met with Kiplinger, whom I knew through his sons Knight and Todd, to learn his secrets of concise summary reporting. He explained how they created brief paragraphs that consisted of only three or four short sentences, some of which were actually incomplete and separated by ellipses:

> *Suicide bombing on the West Bank. . . . Six dead, 50 wounded. . . . Israeli army on alert. . . . No further information.*

We changed the format of the summary, and the analysts and duty officers did their best to emulate Kiplinger's style. The Sit Room has continued to use that style through the present.

When Reagan traveled, the Situation Room organized the flow of routine presidential reporting to his location, just as it has done for all previous and succeeding presidents. At Reagan's ranch in Santa Barbara, California, WHCA manned a communications center, to which we sent, by secure fax, all of the daily reports. The military aide to the President who was on duty picked up the package and delivered it to the President. If the President had questions, the aide passed them to either the duty officers or the NSC representative who accompanied the President on the trip. WHCA had the same system at LBJ's ranch and at Clinton's beach house on Martha's Vineyard.

Rosanne O'Hara, an analyst from NSA, stayed busy writing the daily summary and spot reports during the second Reagan term, a time when kidnappings in the Middle East happened at an alarming frequency. She knew that lives were at risk and that her readers valued quick reporting. O'Hara recalled:

> I remember one instance—the first day Howard Baker, President Reagan's new chief of staff, came on board—when I quickly wrote up a Sit Room note on a fast-breaking event in the Middle East and delivered it upstairs before the morning meeting. I ran up the back stairs and introduced myself to Mr. Baker while trying to catch my breath. He grabbed the paper and walked away and I followed him, thinking he might have a question, through a door to what I thought was his office. It was not his office—it was a little known bathroom in the West Wing. I almost died. But he got his information ASAP!

O'Hara recalled another time when she made an unusual delivery of a Situation Room note. "I took a report to General Powell [Colin Powell, Reagan's last national security adviser] at his home on the weekend. I rang and rang his bell, but no one came to the door. Heading back to the car, I jumped when I heard his familiar voice—he was right there in the driveway, working under the hood of an old Volvo."

= = =

"Kevin, this is George. Christianne Amanpour is on CNN reporting from the town that you told me was obscured by cloud cover and the sun is shining in her face."

Kevin was Kevin O'Connell who was part of the special reporting cell in the Sit Room during the Persian Gulf War. George was George H. W. Bush, 41st President of the United

States. "During both the air and ground campaigns in Iraq, we briefed President Bush every morning on the status of the fighting," said O'Connell. "He asked detailed questions, especially about intelligence collection systems. I had told him that morning that a specific target was cloud-covered and unavailable for satellite imaging. Just thirty minutes after he went back upstairs, he called down and told me about the CNN report. He laughed, so I didn't think it was a 'gotcha.' Besides, I think he knew how hard it was to predict the weather."

The Gulf War severely tested all the watch centers in Washington, but it was especially hard for the Situation Room because of Bush's habits and style. As Vice President, he frequently called for updates, and the duty officers almost fought to pick up the phone first so they could talk to him. He was always gracious and surprisingly informal and he continued that style as President. But his calls increased in frequency and detail during the war, and the duty officer and analysts scrambled to keep up with his needs.

"At first, we were hard-pressed to answer his questions about the details regarding national intelligence collection assets [in other words, satellites]," recalled O'Connell. "He wanted to know if the such-and-such system could do this-and-that, but the people who operated those resources wouldn't tell us that kind of detail. Finally, Bob Gates, Scowcroft's deputy, had to intervene in the intelligence community on our behalf, reassuring the people that we had a legitimate need to know."

According to O'Connell, the Situation Room also had trouble following the progress of the ground war because they were kept in the dark about the specific objectives. That didn't stop Bush from calling to ask for progress reports. "We were in deep trouble, until someone, I think Colin Powell, 'accidentally' left a map in the Sit Room that made us smarter," said O'Connell. "Then we could call NMCC and ask the right questions."

Although Colin Powell, Dick Cheney, and Brent Scowcroft

briefed the President regularly during the Gulf War, Bush still either called the duty officer early every morning or went downstairs for a personal briefing, usually between 4:00 and 5:00 A.M. Kevin O'Connell and his reporting partner, John Montgomery, prepared for that by laying out on a desk all the materials that they knew he would ask about. "We had had all the available intelligence reports—SIGINT [signals intelligence], HUMINT [human intelligence], and imagery, then a pile of reports on military movements, and another on diplomatic issues and foreign reactions."

Bush welcomed CIA briefers into the Oval Office, continuing a practice that he had observed during the eight years he was Vice President. The briefers delivered the PDB directly to Bush, in contrast to the Reagan years.

= = =

Situation Room reporting continued in a similar fashion after Clinton's election, but, again, with a few changes. Neil O'Leary, the Situation director during the transition from Bush to Clinton, sent a folder up to Tony Lake each day for the President. He said that he put the Sit Room Summary on top, followed by the State and DIA reports, as well as other intelligence community products. A CIA briefer brought the PDB to the White House and waited in the Sit Room for his audience with Clinton, and sometimes the wait was a long one.

Walter Pincus reported in great detail in a 1994 *Washington Post* article how Bill Clinton initially entertained daily oral briefings from CIA, but then later cancelled the meetings in favor of just reading the PDB. Pincus also wrote that that the intelligence community felt Clinton's cancellation of the formal CIA briefing showed a lack of interest in foreign policy. Tony Lake said that Clinton did have trouble finding time for the CIA briefer, but that the President always read the PDB.

O'Leary recalled the shift in the importance of different

sources used in the reports during the late 1980s and early 1990s.

"We witnessed the disintegration of the Soviet Union, the fall of the Berlin Wall, and the raising of the Iron Curtain," said O'Leary. "We went from digging for information in the closed society of the Soviet Union to a glut of information. That sea change made information from the news media more important. The news media drove our reporting." Lake echoed that theme when he said that CNN had become so important that he wished, in retrospect, that he had asked CIA to add analysis of top news stories to the PDB.

The Situation Room and the other Washington operations centers acknowledged the virtual explosion of technology developments associated with the growth of the information superhighway in the 1990s. While the LDX revolutionized the shuffling of paper around town in the 1970s, electronic file transfer and email helped the Situation Room make another leap forward in information handling twenty years later.

"Just like the Russians, we never gave up anything that worked," said Kevin Cosgriff, director from 1997 to 1999. "But we also developed a pretty robust capability to receive and disseminate most of our products electronically." The agencies that sent regular reports to the President began to also send them electronically, in addition to the traditional hand-carried or faxed copies. In some instances, some reports were merely a fax or PDF file, but others were word-processing documents that could be manipulated after receipt. The Sit Room also expanded the sure NSC network so traveling staff members could access the NSC local area network as if they were at the White House.

The Internet not only brought new sources of information for alerting and reporting, it also ushered in a new mindset to the process of disseminating intelligence product. Begun in 1994 as a secure version of the Internet, Intelink's creators designed it to operate just the way the World Wide Web did, but separately. Intelink uses the same technology and user interface as the Internet; the DCI declared it in 1994 as "the strategic direction for all intelligence dissemination." All of the main intelligence agencies, DoD commands, law enforcement agencies, and other selected government offices are participants in Intelink. Users log on with passwords that permit access to only those classification levels for which the user is authorized. The most common use of Intelink is basic research on issues emerging on the horizon, allowing an analyst to search for recent imagery, studies, and technical information. Elliot Powell, Sit Room director during 1999–2001, said the Intelink was a useful tool for the duty officers.

Just as the Situation Room sought technologies to help them move words, they also installed a system to disseminate images to White House customers via their desktop computers. In 2001, they purchased and installed a commercially available system from V-Brick Systems that permitted the duty officers to broadcast television-quality MPEG-1 video from satellite feeds, intelligence imagery, or even CNN in real time or on-demand video clips.

President George W. Bush chose to have CIA brief him directly every day, just as it had served his father. The Situation Room staff also sends him their daily summaries, as well as passing on other summaries from DIA, State, and Defense.

After 9-11, President Bush changed his daily intelligence briefing and PDB routine. The *Washington Post's* Pincus, who must have a good source for PDB matters, reported again in May 2002 about sensitive reporting to the President. According to Pincus, the CIA briefer is joined by a representative from the FBI, as well as some of Bush's national security advisers— the DCI, director of the FBI, Dr. Rice, and Vice President Cheney—and the subject matter is far wider in range than before the 2001 terrorist attacks. The PDB process caught the public's attention when the news media reported in May 2002 that on August 6, 2001, the PDB reported that al Qaeda terrorists might attempt to hijack an airplane, a revelation that sparked a brouhaha about what the President knew and when he knew it.

8

PERSONNEL

Ringside Seats

"The President and Mrs. Clinton request the honor of your presence at the Kennedy Center. . . ."

So read a line on the back of a ticket for a seat in the President's Box in the Kennedy Center Concert Hall. Many White House employees are invited to request tickets in the box for events that the President or his family do not attend. The receptionist in the lobby of the West Wing distributes the tickets in a fairly even-handed manner that gives everyone a chance for seats in the box over time. Tony Campanella, a duty officer during the Clinton administration, remembered how he used two tickets to the President's Box.

"I met a girl, who later became my wife, at an art show at the Corcoran Gallery across the street from the White House," Campanella said. "I wanted to ask her out on a date and thought that an evening in the President's Box at the Kennedy Center would impress her. Well, I sent one of the tickets to her and she was impressed."

Later, Campanella proposed to that same young woman, Susan, in the Rose Garden. He arranged for her to visit the

West Wing on a spring evening in April 1999, then walked with her to the Rose Garden, quiet and empty in the gathering dusk.

"We sat on a bench, talking and enjoying all the flowers," Campanella said. "I brought out the ring and proposed. Luckily she accepted and while we hugged each other, Betty Currie, President Clinton's secretary, walked by. She was clearly perplexed, but didn't stop walking. I went up to see her the next morning and explained what we were doing and she thought it was great."

Currie gained a great deal of unwanted notoriety during the Clinton–Monica Lewinski scandal by appearing to facilitate the liaison between the President and a young White House intern. Perhaps she became used to seeing "cupids" at work in the West Wing. Campanella described what happened next.

"During my time in the Situation Room, the NSC staff arranged for duty officers departing at the end of their assignment and their families to attend President Clinton's Saturday morning radio address, then have a photograph taken with the President," said Campanella. "When it was my turn, I introduced Susan to the President and told him about how I proposed to her in the Rose Garden and that Betty had caught us. He was speechless at first and said he couldn't believe it, but then told us it was wonderful."

As noted before, when the subject of the White House Situation Room comes up, most people envision a war room in the bowels of the White House in which the President weighs his options during national crises. But if you listen to the voices of those who have depended on the Sit Room, from presidents on down, the true essence of the facility, its enduring character, is in the people who work there. Henry Kissinger, who called the conference room "uncomfortable, unaesthetic and essentially oppressive," praised the staff in a January 1977 letter to Situation Room director Jim Fazio. "As I leave government I can think of no group of people who have served with as much loyalty, professionalism and dedication as the men and women of the Situation Room. . . . I will never forget what you have done."

Kissinger later reiterated his regard for the Situation Room staff: "I took them for granted, which is a high compliment."

Most staff members have been young and just starting their careers in government service, but all have been professionals, working hard over the years to set the gold standard for customer service in the White House. Former President George Bush gave me his view of the Sit Room staff during the first year of his son's presidency.

"The 'young folks' are dedicated to their work. Old or young, they always impressed me as very eager to give the President or Vice President whatever information was needed regardless of the time of day or night. There was a great esprit de corps in that Sit Room. I hope there still is. They work long hours, come from different agencies, but they all are truly dedicated and they impressed me as knowing what they are doing."

$$= = =$$

From the beginning, national security agencies, primarily CIA, State, Defense, NSA, DIA, and the military services, have seconded or detailed people to the White House in order to staff the Situation Room. The communications technicians are all members of WHCA, a military unit that is part of the Defense Communications Agency. The Executive Office of the President (EOP) is the bureaucratic term for the government unit that contains the President and his immediate staff. The EOP allocates only one or two billets (personnel slots) for Situation Room staff members. The duty officers, analysts, and the director have always been on loan from another agency, which funds their salaries and benefits. There are several reasons for this practice.

First, it helps keep the EOP budget as small as possible. There are political risks associated with large presidential staffs—no president wants to seem surrounded by what appears to be a palace staff with layers of retinue and handholders. So a lot of people who work at the White House are not on the EOP payroll for bureaucratic and political reasons.

Second, if the duty officers were hired for permanent positions, they might settle in for the long haul, send out deep, bureaucratic roots, and become part of the unambitious, self-centered lot that can be found in any government agency. They might begin to find the years of shift work to be so onerous that their "can-do" spirit wanes. Also, since they are on loan, the national security adviser can "un-loan" them in a flash if they are not up to the task or suffer a near-fatal lack of judgment. Uprooting a bureaucrat who doesn't want to leave is tough going, even if reason, common sense, and the Marines are on your side.

Last, the agencies that contribute people to the Sit Room staff recognize the immense value of having one of their own working in the White House. A duty officer returns to his parent agency with much broader horizons, seasoned by real-world challenges. But these assignments also allow the creation both of useful feedback loops between watch centers and of an extremely valuable back channel for information exchange when interagency coordination becomes poisoned by turf wars or plain old bureaucratic inertia. A Soviet ballistic missile submarine suffered an explosion in one of its missile tubes off the U.S. East Coast in 1986. My Navy duty officer was able to get a photo of the stricken submarine sent over immediately from the Office of Naval Intelligence. We were able to show it to President Reagan twenty-four hours before the bureaucracy churned one out.

When the Situation Room opened for business in May 1961, McGeorge Bundy and Bromley Smith arranged for CIA employees to become the first duty officers. Walt Rostow, who was Bundy's deputy at the time, said that CIA was a natural choice for the source of manpower—the people already had security clearances and they were thought to be apolitical. Tazewell Shepard, then Kennedy's naval aide and the initial, nominal head of the new facility, said that choosing CIA personnel dodged the interservice rivalry that often flared up between Kennedy's semiautonomous military aides.

This feeling did not, however, stop Kenneth O'Donnell, Kennedy's close adviser, from asking the Defense Department to designate military personnel from each service to serve as "augmentees" in the Situation Room during crises. In a February 1963 memo to DoD, O'Donnell noted that the Cuban Missile Crisis the previous year proved that the existing staff was insufficient and asked that each service be ready to send experienced personnel from their respective war rooms to the Situation Room, if needed. The NSC never exercised this manning option, and McGeorge Bundy rescinded the requirement in a 1964 memo.

For much of the 1960s and 1970s, most of the duty officers were drawn from CIA ranks, with most of them from the office that ran the CIA Operations Center. CIA established a career path for watch standers that fostered repeated assignments to the White House. After several years of seasoning at the CIA Ops Center, a person was sent to the Sit Room to become a junior duty officer. He then returned to CIA, gained more experience, and later served as a senior duty officer in the Sit Room. I knew several CIA employees who spent the majority of their career standing watches at either the CIA or the White House.

A dangerous espionage case jolted the duty officers from CIA in the late 1970s. William Kampiles worked as a watch stander at the CIA operations center from March to November 1977. When he resigned, he took with him a manual that described the operations of the KH-11 imaging satellite and sold it to the Soviet Union for three thousand dollars. During the ensuing investigation, the CIA called back to headquarters those employees assigned to the Situation Room for questioning. Dennis Chapman, then the Sit Room director, said that none of his duty officers was involved. A federal court convicted Kampiles of espionage and sentenced him to prison for forty years.

NSA began sending an analyst to the Situation Room in the mid-1960s, first as a near-daily visitor, then on a full-time assignment. Initially, NSA wanted to help the duty officers and, more important, the NSC staff better understand and employ the huge array of NSA products. David McManis, the director of the Situation Room under Nixon, was the first NSA analyst detailed to the Sit Room. Since then, NSA has always contributed analysts and, in addition to McManis, another director.

The State Department has assigned young Foreign Service officers to the Situation Room, usually for a one-year assignment immediately after they completed a twelve-month tour in the State Operations Center. They have brought a wonderfully broad knowledge of world affairs to the Situation Room and a sound understanding of the international diplomatic process and protocol that can mystify duty officers with narrower experience. A charge d'affaires delivered a demarche?

Bonnie Glick, a Foreign Service officer on loan from State, served as a duty officer from 1997 to 1999. "When I walked in, I was met by alien beings—intelligence types and military officers," said Glick. "I was on a team with an intelligence analyst from NSA and a Navy officer. As a diplomat, I was used to talking to people, but NSA is such a secretive agency that he was really closed-mouthed. The Navy guy was so stern at first, that I asked him if he had to rise to a certain rank before he was issued a sense of humor."

When I became director, personnel from CIA, NSA, and

State manned the Situation Room. I set out to recruit a representative from each military service, not only to create five watch teams instead of four, but also to develop the broadest knowledge base possible in the Sit Room. There had been cases when the CIA and State duty officers missed the significance of a military incident, just as an Army officer could have missed a diplomatic innuendo. This arrangement continues to the present and now includes the Coast Guard.

Lieutenant Commander Gerry McCabe, Kennedy's assistant naval aide, was the first officer in charge of the Situation Room. While he was the nominal head of the facility, most of the direction and supervision of the duty officers came from Bromley Smith, the executive secretary of the NSC. McCabe's successor was Commander Oliver Hallett, whose position was eliminated after Kennedy's assassination. Smith and Bundy named Art McCafferty, from CIA, the first director of the Situation Room in 1963. Since then, CIA has provided a second director, Joyce Harmon, and NSA, two—David McManis and Manny Rubio. There have been two directors from State, Jim Fazio and Dennis Chapman, and one from DIA, Neil O'Leary. One director was an Air Force officer, Paul LeBras, and one came from the Army, Jim Reed. The Navy has provided the last three consecutive directors—Kevin Cosgriff, Elliott Powell, and Deborah Loewer.

Under Clinton's national security advisers, the Situation Room director also traveled with the President on domestic trips, serving as the NSC representative in the traveling party. The national security adviser, his deputy, or the NSC executive secretary had usually performed that role in past administrations.

"I just took advantage of the available manpower," said Tony Lake. "I didn't need to fly with the President to Denver, when the Situation Room director or the NSC executive secretary could easily relay information from me to President Clinton, if required."

Elliot Powell said that when traveling with the President, he had to concentrate not on the purpose of the trip, but on developments away from the President. "I had to keep my focus on the whole world, while the rest of the party on Air Force One was zeroed in on the scheduled events," said Powell. He also had to keep his concentration late into the night.

"We were on our way back to Washington late one night when the President's aide came to the back of the plane where I was trying to catch a nap," said Powell. "He said the President wanted to play some Hearts and asked if I was up for it. President Clinton liked to play cards to relax, but he was serious about the game. Even though I was pretty tired that night, I took the President at his own game."

An assignment to the Situation Room has traditionally provided a boost to a young person's career whether he was an intelligence analyst at DIA, a Navy officer, or a linguist at NSA. The State Department assigned Roman Popadiuk, a Foreign Service officer, to the Situation Room when I was the director. After his tour was up, he stayed at the White House working in the Press Office. He later rose to become deputy press secretary to President Bush and principal spokesman for the NSC. Bush later appointed Roman to be the first U.S. ambassador to Ukraine.

Virtually everyone assigned to the Situation Room has enjoyed the experience. Fred Wergeles, an analyst from CIA during the Reagan years, said that every day was exciting. "Unless you are driving at Indianapolis or throwing touchdown passes in the Super Bowl, it's hard to beat working in the Situation Room. Every day was an adrenaline rush."

Bob O'Hara, an analyst in the late 1980s, said that working in the White House was a lifelong dream. "I remember telling my parents on one of our frequent visits to Washington from

Ohio that I was going to live in Washington when I grew up and I was determined to work in the White House. I never lost the feeling that working there was an honor and a privilege."

A Situation Room assignment is not necessarily risk-free, however. Tony Lake, Clinton's first national security adviser, recognized the stress under which the duty officers can be placed if they are caught in bureaucratic tug-of-wars. "I often had to ask the duty officers to seek information from their home agencies in a manner that created tensions between the individual and his permanent boss," Lake said. "Usually, those situations arose when the duty officers were merely cutting through red tape on my behalf, but I didn't want their careers jeopardized just because they were doing what I had directed."

Tensions also arose when these relatively junior duty officers interacted with officials at other agencies who were vastly superior in rank or title. Military officers and enlisted personnel working in the Situation Room never identified themselves as such when talking to the Pentagon for fear of an unknowing general pulling rank on them and not answering the President's question. For the same reason, they never wore their uniforms while on duty. In fact, none of the military assigned to the White House, save the President's aides and the White House Social Aides, ever wore uniforms. If they did, the place would look like an armed camp, not quite the perception that a civilian commander in chief wants projected.

Kevin O'Connell, an analyst in the Situation Room under former President Bush, told a story about two nervous generals from the Pentagon pacing the floor in anticipation of briefing the President in the conference room. "One of the military duty officers, an Army captain who spoke to Bush routinely, advised the generals to take it easy and that the President always put people at ease," O'Connell said. "They gave him a look that clearly said, 'How could anyone so young know anything about briefing the President?'"

Much of the success that the duty officers and analysts have achieved in the Situation Room can be credited to the fact that they have checked their egos at the door. I told a new officer reporting for duty that there were a lot of important people in the White House, but he wasn't one of them. Most knew that already, but all soon realized that all aspects of their performance hinged on an enthusiastic, service-oriented attitude. Their friendly, can-do spirit stands in marked contrast to the only other group of young people in the White House, interns and junior secretaries. Perhaps the following is a stereotype, but most of that crowd seemed to be daughters of wealthy campaign contributors. Some seemed carried away with their positions and eager to climb the ladders of power and influence, ambitions that are not uncommon in the West Wing.

"The Situation Room folks had no ax to grind," said Bob Gates, who, as DCI, contributed some of the duty officers and, as deputy national security adviser, depended on them daily. "They were professionals who did not have their own agenda and thus were not selective in their actions." I can remember only one exception to Gates' assessment. A duty officer who worked for me slipped a note into President Reagan's folder one morning in which he assailed the President's position on Ferdinand Marcos of the Philippines. Placing his own feelings ahead of the professional neutrality required for the job was an egregious error in judgment. I sent him back to CIA immediately.

Bud McFarlane, who served Nixon, Ford, and Reagan, said the Situation Room's greatest strength was its personnel. "Their sense of duty, and I know that sounds hackneyed, was impressive. The Situation Room could have been a place for opportunists, for hubris, and for personal gain, but I never saw it. No one ever asked me for a promotion or complained; they were the most professional, selfless, and loyal public servants I have ever encountered."

Each duty officer arrived at the Situation Room with a basic knowledge of national intelligence resources, experience in briefing and writing reports, and a general appreciation of current international issues. But as the junior duty officer on a team of three—two junior and one senior duty officer, he or she quickly got the firehose treatment in learning the details of everything going on around the world. Bonnie Glick remembered the steep learning curve.

"We not only had to adjust to each other, but also we had to, in the words of my boss, Kevin Cosgriff, 'Get smart really fast,'" said Glick. "I had never read that many intelligence reports at State, so it took me a while to understand the formats. On the other hand, the military officers thought that some of the State cables were silly. They didn't understand that embassies, in an attempt to get someone in Washington to read their cables, used catchy titles or a tongue-in-cheek phrase."

Please bear in mind that this team of three young people does not stand alone on the precipice of national disaster—there are several other watch centers screening the same material, and the Sit Room director is but a phone call away. Nevertheless, they quickly learn what they know and don't know. There is no sin in not being able to answer a question if you have to beat the bushes for the information, but woe unto those who try winging it at the White House. There is no room for guesses. Former President Bush told me once that "the Situation Room people were not afraid to tell the President, 'I don't know'; but they didn't have to do that very often."

=== === ===

At first, in 1961, there were just three senior duty officers assigned to the Situation Room, all from CIA. Each worked a twenty-four hour shift, every third day. From 9:30 A.M. to 5:00 P.M. they worked in the NSC office in the Executive Office Building, sorting through incoming material on behalf of the senior NSC staff members who had offices in that building.

The President's assistant naval aide worked in the Situation Room during the day, supported by another person from the White House Military Office and a WHCA liaison officer. They were responsible for alerting during working hours, as well as maintenance and staff support to Bromley Smith and McGeorge Bundy.

During the evening and overnight, the CIA duty officer moved to the Situation Room and screened material hand-carried from the East Wing communications center. He took a nap during the night if things were quiet.

After Kennedy's assassination, Art McCafferty exercised full control of the Situation Room, ending the operations split between the Military Office and the NSC staff. He obtained more duty officers from CIA in order to have a junior duty officer in the Sit Room twenty-four hours a day. Four of them rotated on eight-hour shifts, while the senior duty officers kept the twenty-four-hour-shift cycle. This arrangement continued until the Reagan administration, when the two different watch rotations were combined into four teams of three, two juniors and a senior. I recruited more duty officers so that we could create five teams of three, each working twelve-hour shifts. A team worked a week of days, a week of nights, then a week of eight-hour shifts during regular working hours, a period that was great for training. The arrangement also provided the director with "surge" capability during crises.

McCafferty added the NSA analyst who worked during the day; a second analyst came later, often drawn from DIA. David McManis added a deputy director position in 1969, recruiting Jim Fazio from the Intelligence and Research Bureau at State.

Ralph Sigler has been the deputy director of the Situation Room since 1981, a remarkable twenty-one-year run. He arrived in the Sit Room first as a WHCA communications technician during the Nixon administration, then, after retiring from the Army, joined the NSC staff as a civilian employee. He has seen just about everything there is to see in the Situation Room, but declined to be interviewed.

Late in the Reagan administration, the national security adviser tasked the analysts in the Crisis Management Center to provide assistance to both the Situation Room and NSC staff members. The Bush administration eliminated those positions in 1989, but the group of computer technicians in the CMC lived on and continued to provide computer assistance to the Situation Room. They became the core of a new office in the 1990s, NSC Systems and Technical Planning, a group of eighteen people who guide information technology operations for both the NSC staff and the Sit Room. The director of the Situation Room became the head of that group.

Life as a Situation Room duty officer or analyst certainly has its pluses and minuses. The main plus is having a ringside seat at one of the greatest shows on earth. You work at the best address in town, 1600 Pennsylvania Avenue, and while you are pretty low on the totem pole, at least you've got a perch on that fascinating pole. The work is intellectually challenging and extraordinarily fulfilling. Even a duty officer can have an impact on the world stage. Bob Gates recalled a critical point in the Gulf War when President Bush was on the phone with French President François Mitterand, attempting to convince the French that it was time to start the ground war with Iraq. "The senior duty officer ran upstairs to my office with a report that Iraq had set fire to Kuwaiti oil wells," said Gates. "I quickly took that report to the Oval Office and slipped it in front of the President when he was on the phone with Mitterand. The French president immediately agreed to launch the ground war."

There are some White House perks that trickle down to the Situation Room staff, though not nearly what the more senior staff enjoys. As Tony Campanella knows, a duty officer can get an occasional ticket in the President's Box, watch ceremonies from the front row, and attend the White House Christmas parties and Easter Egg Roll. The President usually entertains winning sports teams, and joining those events was a highlight for me. President Reagan hosted a reception in the Rose Garden for the 1986 World Series champs, the New York Mets. I took my two boys to the ceremony and they got autographs by the fistful. When my oldest son, Carter, drifted away in search of Dwight Gooden's signature, I called out his name several times to ask him to stay with me. Gary Carter, the Met's All Star catcher, turned around and said that he would be happy to answer any questions, but please call him Gary.

Some presidents have gone out of their way to drop by the Situation Room to chat with the unsung and usually unseen duty officers. President George H. W. Bush was best at this, but his son has carried on the family tradition by recognizing that a quick "thumbs up" or a "Howdy" does wonders for Sit Room morale. Clinton visited less often, and Reagan, who appeared to do nothing spontaneously, waved and said hello as he entered the conference room.

David Sedney, a duty officer from State who worked for both Presidents Reagan and George H. W. Bush, said Barbara Bush called the Situation Room one evening, asking if the duty officers were busy. "When the senior duty officer told her that it was a slow watch, she invited whomever could get away to come upstairs to the movie theater and join the First Family," said Sedney. "A couple of people accepted and the Bushes served them popcorn and treated them like family."

Over the years the Situation Room staff has organized parties, luncheons, and dinners in the conference room. We had Thanksgiving dinners while I was there, with everyone bringing a dish to share. Since the duty officers worked around the clock and often missed holidays at home, they wanted to celebrate Thanksgiving with their "second family" in the Sit Room.

In 1986, the Mess roasted the turkey for us. Rosanne O'Hara, an analyst from NSA, remembered what happened next. "I rushed home from the White House after the Mess cooked it, garnished it with sage leaves and rosemary, and placed it on a huge platter and rushed back," O'Hara said. "The trip went great until I turned into the Southwest Gate. The turkey slid off its platter into my back seat, garnish flew everywhere, and the Secret Service guard dogs went crazy with the aroma in my car. I jumped out of my car, showed my badge to the guards, but had to grab the turkey, the sage, and rosemary before the dogs did. With turkey juice all over me, I wobbled into the Sit Room and joined the rest of the hungry gang, never divulging this little episode until now. The Sit Room always delivers!"

On the minus side, the watch routine is a tough schedule. Changing one's sleep period back and forth from night to day is hard on the body. Studies have shown that staying on the night shift for long periods of time is better for you physically than a week of night shifts followed by a week of days. But the duty officers preferred the short cycles. Some observers have suggested that Situation Room duty officers have always been relatively young because shift work and middle age are incompatible.

"After I left the White House, people often asked how I could possibly leave such an interesting job," said Bob O'Hara. "I told them that two-plus years on the graveyard shift—which turned into a six-day-a-week job in the Bush White House—was physically and mentally demanding. Plus my wife and I were starting a family and I wanted to see them once in a while. I lost a lot of vacation during those years, but I was working in the White House, so it balanced out."

O'Hara, who left NSA and is now a lawyer in Connecticut, recalled how a Philippines coup attempt postponed his transition from Situation Room analyst to the legal field.

"President Bush was in Europe for a NATO summit, so when we heard about the coup attempt, I stayed in the Situation Room with Vice President Dan Quayle for almost a double shift," said O'Hara. "I took the LSAT [Law School Admissions Test] the next day on only two hours of sleep. I didn't score high enough for acceptance to Georgetown Law, but I was admitted the following year after retesting."

Working in the West Wing is heady stuff, but getting there isn't so glamorous. Parking has always been hard for the duty officers. On weekdays, they parked on the Ellipse, south of the White House, but there were never enough parking passes to go around. So the departing team had to go out to their cars toward the end of their shift, get the pass from their cars, then leave the passes at the Southwest Gate for the oncoming shift. On weekends, however, the watch teams and the analysts were allowed to park on the White House grounds.

Bob O'Hara, who came to work at 3:00 A.M., said that finding a good parking spot on the Ellipse was the easy part. The hard part was walking from his car to the gate. "Invariably, there were street people, sleeping, drinking, or trying to panhandle or sell drugs just outside the White House grounds, said O'Hara. "I remember one guy trying to intimidate me before I got out of the car . . . until I stood up—I was 6'4" and 240 at the time. He took off like a scared rabbit, but it left me uneasy because it showed how vulnerable you were if someone had a weapon. The Secret Service used to get a kick out me getting hassled on the Ellipse; I guess they were bored on post."

The other challenge came from the legendary White House rats. "I often saw them scurrying around West Exec headed toward the West Wing or the South Lawn," said O'Hara. "They looked big enough to be muskrats, but their tails gave them away. Even the Secret Service guard dogs were afraid of them."

The other O'Hara, Rosanne—yes, they are married and more on that later—also remembers the rats. "One rat jumped off the curb just outside the Southwest Gate, she said. "I jumped and turned in fright and apparently entertained the Secret Service officers at the gate. They recorded my dance with a video camera, so as I entered the West Wing, I got a standing ovation from the Secret Service guys inside."

When some of the old temporary buildings near the White House were torn down in the 1970s, Sally Botsai said that some homeless rats took up residence in the White House. "We heard them scurrying around above the ceiling tiles and often wondered whether they ever made an appearance at formal dinners upstairs," Botsai said. "Some of the lesser creatures, the cockroaches, were an ever-present nuisance in the Sit Room, as well. They especially enjoyed the glue holding telephone books together, and sometimes ate the plastic telephone wire coverings."

═══ ═══ ═══

A more serious downside to working in the Sit Room is the stress of a crisis—phones ringing incessantly, people demanding answers, deadlines to meet, and all of this on a lousy five-hour nap before coming to work at 6:00 P.M. And at least once, workers in the Situation Room have faced deadly peril. On September 11, 2001, authorities believed a fourth plane was headed for either the White House or the Capitol. Although the airliner crashed in Pennsylvania before reaching Washington, everyone evacuated the White House. Everyone, except the Situation Room staff.

Jim Fazio, director during the Nixon and Ford administrations, recalled a bomb threat that caused the Secret Service to order an evacuation of the West Wing, or at least most of it. "They forgot about the Sit Room and we kept working, blissfully ignorant of the flap upstairs."

Presidential scandals have been tough on the staff. Sally Botsai remembers that one of the saddest periods of her tour in the Sit Room occurred during Watergate. As the situation worsened, people in all the offices of the West Wing turned

their televisions to the steady stream of damaging developments. The duty officers watched their TV as well.

"The atmosphere in the White House was subdued, and
people gathered outside the gates and fences trying to glimpse
at those coming and going," Botsai said. "Most seemed pen-
sive, sober, quiet."

On the day before President Nixon resigned, Botsai said that
the Situation Room began receiving reports that the White
House press corps had been locked in the Press Briefing Theater. "There was an air of indignation, as though they were
being punished," recalled Botsai. "About that time, I received
a call from the Secret Service to the effect that we, too, were
asked to stay in our spaces. We were kept behind closed doors
for thirty minutes until the Secret Service called again to say
that we could come out. By this time, the press was in high
dudgeon, not knowing that all offices had been sequestered."

Botsai said they later learned that the reason for this was
that President Nixon wanted to walk through the White House
for the last time as President without seeing anyone, hence the
Secret Service lockup of all the offices.

"The next morning we were invited to the East Room,
where he and his family assembled for his farewell speech to
the White House staff," said Botsai. "It was an awkward, emo-
tional speech, with his family and the President himself in
tears. After that, the party walked to the South Lawn, where
the helicopter awaited them. The last wave I saw from the bal-
cony was that of Henry Kissinger."

Gerald Ford became President at noon the same day in the
East Room. "Brent Scowcroft called a meeting of the entire
NSC staff, saying that he expected them to carry on without
any changes," said Botsai. "I remember how gloomy it was that
day, for by then it was pouring rain."

The Iran-Contra affair also brought stress and pressures to
the Sit Room staff. The duty officers were shocked that one of

their favorite NSC staffers, Ollie North, and their boss, national security adviser John Poindexter, were forced to leave the White House. Although both were convicted of felonies, the judgments against North and Poindexter were later overturned. North kept my staff and me in the dark about his covert activities to support the Contras in Nicaragua, but that didn't stop the FBI from emptying my safe one day, searching for evidence of wrongdoing in the Situation Room. While Frank Carlucci, the next national security adviser, dismissed a sizable portion of the NSC staff in the aftermath of the Iran-Contra scandal, investigators did not implicate anyone in the Situation Room for inappropriate actions.

Vice President Bush made a point to visit the duty officers during the height of the Iran-Contra tension, again demonstrating his widely recognized concern for the individuals who worked for him. His pep talks helped the staff make a smooth transition to the new national security adviser.

During the Monica Lewinski scandal and President Clinton's subsequent impeachment, the Situation Room duty officers weathered the maelstrom well. They certainly did not escape the daily barrage of news, speculation, and innuendo, but they kept their energy on the job at hand. Kevin Cosgriff, then the director, kept his staff focused by reminding them that life and death in the Balkans would continue, Saddam Hussein would keep harassing UN inspectors, and terrorists would still try to kill innocent people.

"Sandy Berger told us that the world would keep going during all of that, so we had to keep doing our job," said Tony Campanella, a duty officer at the time. "Luckily, there was a lot going on around the world in those days, so we had plenty to keep our minds off the impeachment process. But since we watched CNN all the time, it was hard to keep from being distracted by their constant reporting of the impeachment process."

═ ═ ═

Rosanne O'Hara worked as an analyst in the Situation Room for two years, alternating between the early morning and day shifts. On the early shift, she edited and wrote the Sit Room Morning Summary; on the day shift, the Evening Summary. While at the White House, she began dating her future husband, Bob O'Hara, who worked at NSA's National SIGINT Operations Center (NSOC). They married while she was still in the Situation Room, then Bob replaced Rosanne as the resident NSA analyst. As Roseanne told it:

> I was the first intelligence analyst to have a wedding shower in the White House Situation Room.
>
> Bob and I exchanged information over the secure phone during fast-breaking situations and I got SIGINT confirmation of events from NSOC faster than anyone else. On the other hand, the Situation Room connection could have ruined our relationship later on because I had to train him (or as he says, he had to endure my training) in the Sit Room. When we were on the same shift, things worked fine. But often a bombing or two prolonged his shift and we didn't see each other for days. But now, almost fifteen years later, we are happily married and proud to say that we have a great letter from President Reagan celebrating our marriage and a letter from President Bush on the birth of our first child.

Another couple, a Marine intelligence officer and a CIA analyst, met and married in the Situation Room. Because of the husband's activities at CIA, the couple asked me to withhold their names.

9

THE WHITE HOUSE HELP DESK

"Hit the F7 button, Mr. President."

Kevin O'Connell, a Situation Room analyst, made that suggestion to President George H. W. Bush with his fingers crossed, hoping it would help Bush fix a word-processing problem on his computer.

"The Secret Service called the Sit Room early one morning and asked if anyone could come upstairs and help 'someone' with a computer problem," said O'Connell. "When I got to the top of the stairs, the agent told me that the President was waiting for me in the Oval Office. I hadn't known it was the President with the problem, so I immediately began to question my computer fix-it abilities."

President Bush told O'Connell that he had lost a memo he had been writing. "Since most of the computers in the West Wing were just like ours in the Sit Room, I guessed that some extraneous lines had obscured his text. When that happened to me, I would hit the F7 button to delete the unnecessary text. As I held my breath, the President pushed the F7 button and his memo magically reappeared on his screen. He was delighted."

This is but one example of the many requests for help the duty officers have fielded since 1961. Members of every administration since then have gone to the Situation Room seeking all kinds of assistance. Staffers see it as a 24/7 Help Desk, always on call, night or day; and the cheerful, can-do attitude of the Sit Room staff simply increases the number of queries and calls.

The Sit Room's primary customer, and the one who always seems to need service, is the national security adviser. Situation Room staff has always assisted him in ways that are a little out of the ordinary. They have delivered sensitive documents to sensitive places, worked the phones after the NSC secretaries have gone for the day, and generally served as the concierge for the West Wing. Sit Room analyst Sally Botsai recalled a trip to Henry Kissinger's house.

"One morning I went with one of the front office secretaries to Dr. Kissinger's house on an errand," said Botsai. "It was dark when we entered the house and I thought I saw a form on the bed. I gestured to her that we should get out, but she laughed and flicked on the light. The form on the bed was just some rumpled sheets. Henry was nowhere in sight."

The Sit Room was also the temporary repository for gifts that foreign leaders gave President Nixon or Henry Kissinger when they traveled overseas. Botsai remembered that they had gifts—intricate samovars, china, and woodcarvings—stacked everywhere. "The Sit Room also processed some of the correspondence sent to Kissinger, especially from unofficial sources," said Botsai. "Some letters were written by obviously disturbed people, asking that he help them obtain a release from institutions. Women sent him handmade gifts, such as scarves, ties, and drawings, and quite a few sent their pictures, in hopes of attracting the attention of a powerful Washington bachelor."

Christmas gifts for the First Family also accumulated in the

Situation Room during the Kennedy administration. Chuck Enright, a duty officer during those years, recalled acting as one of Santa Claus's elves after President and Mrs. Kennedy had left the White House for their holiday visit to Palm Beach. "Mrs. Kennedy's social secretary called to ask me to select several toys for the President's children from the huge pile that had been brought to the Sit Room. I chose the toys and arranged for them to be sent to Florida."

Closing up the national security adviser's office was another aspect of the Sit Room staff's job. Botsai explained that when Brent Scowcroft was President Ford's national security adviser, he occupied a large corner office on the first floor. He also had a large desk, which Botsai said was the good news. The bad news was that he could put more paper on it. "He had stacks in each corner of the desk, with other stacks lining all the edges except for the space just in front of him," recalled Botsai. "If I had to close up his office at night, I removed the paper piles, each with its own number or label designating its place, and placed them in safes so that they could be returned to the same spot on his desk the next day. Some of the piles were almost a foot high, and there was no clear spot where I would place the morning brief."

When I worked in the Situation Room, people frequently asked for the local time in another country. We had a conversion table, but it was confusing to many of us. I ordered a Geochron clock for the Sit Room, and it quickly became a powerful tool. A rectangular box, about thirty inches wide and eighteen inches high, it displayed a Mercator projection of the world. Superimposed on the surface of the earth was a shadow that indicated what parts of the world were in darkness. The shadow moved in synch with the earth's rotation, the shape of the shadow pattern changing with the seasons. Across the top of the clock were time zone markers, and the International Dateline helped determine when it was tomorrow in Tokyo.

The clock definitely made answering time zone queries much easier.

Paul LeBras, who followed me as director, remembered that it was often the little things, just out of the ordinary, that caused problems:

> Typical was a incident when the duty officer forgot to give Colin Powell a briefcase full of vacation reading for President Reagan who was headed to his ranch in Santa Barbara. Reagan and Powell were already on Air Force One headed west when I realized the problem. I was about to give my deputy Ralph Sigler my credit card and send him to the West Coast on a commercial plane with the briefcase when I heard that an Air Force support plane was due to leave Andrews Air Force Base for Santa Barbara in two hours. We got the briefcase on that plane and I saved my job for another week.

Former duty officers think the Help Desk function peaked during former President Bush's administration. It was not that President Bush needed more help, but that he had a continual dialogue with the duty officers.

"President Bush seemed to get bored on the weekends, especially when he and Mrs. Bush stayed at the White House instead of going to Camp David," recalled Dave Radi, a Navy officer assigned to the Sit Room in the late 1980s. "He would call downstairs and ask if we had anything interesting to read. 'Bring me something to read,' Bush said. 'Do you have any funny cables?' There were several ambassadors that wrote clever cables and we tried to forward them to the President through Brent Scowcroft," said Radi.

The Situation Room was a research source—and more—for the NSC. Tony Lake, Clinton's first national security adviser, recalls his first days in the West Wing. "There is an illusion that, since you won the Presidency, you know everything,"

Lake said. "I guess I wasn't that confident, so I had the Situation Room find every report on Bosnia for the past year or two. I would read the material in the Situation Room or my office on Sundays when no one was around. If I got hungry, I would raid the Sit Room's fridge and hang out down there and talk to the duty officers.

During the second Clinton term, former duty officer Bonnie Glick was a self-described Jewish Mother to the NSC staff in the West Wing.

"Sandy Berger would often work weekends and he didn't want to bring in his secretary on her days off, so we helped him," said Glick. "I could tell when he got grumpy that he was hungry, so I would find something in the Sit Room fridge for him to eat."

The Situation Room staff performed all of these odd jobs— finding magazines for the President, fixing computers, and feeding hungry national security advisers—because they could. They *could do* then, *can do* now, and *will do* tomorrow.

10

THE FUTURE
SITUATION ROOM

The functions of the Situation Room have changed little since its creation in 1961. Although the staff has responded to the increased speed and volume of communications by developing better tools, they still have performed essentially the same activities for more than forty years.

This last chapter is a fictional account of a future crisis as seen through the eyes of the Situation Room duty officers. It is meant to show that however advanced computer and communications systems can become, the human side of the Sit Room remains constant. All characters are fictitious and any resemblance to persons living or dead is coincidental. However, the duty officer's new tools are based on current research and development that experts expect to be available in the near future.

"Crisis Net Alert!"

Mary Simmons, senior duty officer in the White House Situation Room, was eating a sandwich and watching TV in the conference room when she heard the shout and jumped from her chair. She walked quickly to her console in the next room.

The Alert Window on her terminal flashed, "Urgent message from CIA Ops Center—Log onto Crisis Net Conference." The time and date—2235, 20 October 2006—appeared just below the message.

"Pull up Crisis Net," Mary said to Norm Palmer, one of her two junior duty officers.

Norm clicked on the voice icon on his screen, adjusted his headset microphone, and said, "Otto, this is Norm Palmer. Open Crisis Net." A small window opened on his screen and flashed: "Welcome Norman Palmer," indicating that the computer successfully recognized Norm's voice. An experienced duty officer from CIA, Norm watched as the computer system filled his screen with the Crisis Net Videoconference page. Small windows appeared as each Washington watch center logged on the net and the faces of Norm's counterparts filled each window.

While Norm waited for all of the watch centers to join the videoconference, Chuck Holmes, Mary's new junior duty officer, asked, "Who's Otto?"

"When the NSC installed our new computer system, the duty officers started calling it our auto pilot because it performs many of the functions past duty officers had to do manually," said Mary. "'Auto' quickly became 'Otto' and the system's speech recognition adapted to that name. Some of the older duty officers wanted to call it 'Hal,' but not enough people had seen the old movie to understand."

When all of the watch centers were logged on, Norm initiated the meeting because the Situation Room was the default moderator. He switched the conference audio from his headset to his workstation speakers and said, "What's up, CIA?"

"Our people in Tropicland just reported that a coup against President Goodguy is imminent. Colonel Badguy has been leading street demonstrations against Goodguy's government for the past three days, and while the mob is at the gates to the Government House, the colonel has been curiously absent today. We have filed our source's report in Crisis Brief; just click on Tropicland for the full text."

Norm noticed that the frame around the State Department's window blinked, indicating that duty officer wanted to speak. "What do you have, State?"

"As all of you know by reading the cables, our embassy in Palmville has felt that President Goodguy alienated a substantial portion of the country by aligning himself so strongly with the U.S. last year. Badguy is foremost an opportunist, and he may consider the time is right to attempt to unseat Goodguy. NSA, do you know where Badguy is today and what he's doing?"

The NSA duty officer explained that they had been following phone calls from Colonel Badguy's organization, but there had been an abrupt cessation of intercepts today. As NSA briefed everyone on the background of Badguy's communications profile, Mary leaned toward Norm and quietly asked, "Did you activate Multilog?" Norm nodded yes.

Looking at Chuck's face, Mary anticipated his next question. "The system's speech recognition subset can process a dialogue between multiple speakers, a 'multilog,' then furnish us with a text file containing the minutes of the session."

"I have seen nothing on CNN," said the duty officer at the Pentagon. "Have MSNBC or Fox been covering the demonstrations? Should we tip off CNN?"

If any of the cable news channels had been reporting on the situation in Tropicland, all of the duty officers would have seen the coverage. Norm, sensing that the group had run out of facts, asked if anyone had anything else. As all of the negative replies came in, Norm turned to Mary and pointed upstairs. She nodded silently in the affirmative.

"Alright, then, we are going to notify Mr. Pickard," Norm announced to the other duty officers. "I assume you all will also notify your principals. If anyone gets new information that is not distributed to everyone, please post it on the Tropicland page of Crisis Brief and alert everyone. Thanks and good-night."

"Good job, Norm," said Mary. She then put on her headset and said, "Otto, set up a filter for Tropicland. Use the names, locations, dates, and sources in the CIA report in Crisis Brief on the Tropicland page. Check all incoming text, audio, im-ages, and video for links and matches. Activate a continuing Internet search." A window opened on her screen and showed a caricature of a small man—Otto—catching a baseball with his glove, indicating not only that Otto understood, but also that sports metaphors remain unavoidable, even in the White House Situation Room.

"Otto, next job," Mary said to indicate that more instruc-tions would follow. "Search the CNN file for audio or video on President Goodguy, Colonel Badguy, or demonstrations. Check History for past six weeks. Check History for coups in Tropicland. If positive, alert me and queue results in Crisis Brief."

"Otto, next job. Contact Rick White, Daniel Pickard, Jim Bennett, and Stephanie Smith. My message is, 'CIA reports that a possible coup in Tropicland is imminent. Colonel Bad-guy may try to seize power from President Goodguy. No cor-roboration. Details in Crisis Brief; click on Tropicland. Mary Simmons, Situation Room SDO.'"

"Norm, please write a Sit Room Alert Note. Let me know when it's ready."

Chuck's eyes were pretty big by this time, so Mary thought she could spare a few minutes to explain what just happened as she waited for Norm to finish the Alert Note.

"In the old days, the duty officers did all this by phone. They had a NOIWON conference call if NSA issued a CRITIC or if any ops center got wind of a potential crisis. The duty officers then called the NSC staff and the national security adviser by phone and described the situation. Now, Otto handles most of the alerting, screening, and communications chores. Crisis Net is a subset of our computer system, not a separate network like the old, compartmented systems. Instead of a phone call, the first agency with crisis information simply sends an instant message to all the other ops centers. Crisis Net's video conferencing subsystem took the place of the NOIWON conference call. Crisis Net hosts pages for each crisis and each ops center can access those pages rather than each agency sending cables or faxes to each other to share information. Crisis Net feeds Crisis Brief, the primary means of distributing reports on situations. Net and Brief run all the time so we don't have to activate them if a crisis pops up."

"I know that Rick White is our boss and Daniel Pickard is the national security adviser, but who are the other people you sent the alert to?"

Mary explained that Jim Bennett is Pickard's deputy and Stephanie Smith is the senior director for Latin America on the NSC staff. She also told Chuck that she expected Pickard to notify the President.

"What is the filter that you told Otto to set up?" Chuck asked.

"The Sit Room used search engines in the past to catch relevant incoming information on crises, but the new system is much more capable. It uses a process involving associative memory, data extraction, and link detection to screen useful inputs from the rest of incoming information. It takes the key observations from CIA's report on Colonel Badguy's possible coup and searches for matches and links in any data we already have—the History database, or everything we receive now.

"The biggest leap for Otto was image and audio recognition and processing. Once the NSC computer wizards arranged for the necessary bandwidth and storage capabilities, they installed the tools to monitor TV broadcasts, as well as textual inputs. Otto screens CNN, for instance, for images that are on our interest list, comparing incoming images with our interest file. It also converts the TV audio to text, then compares the text to our profiles."

"I guess that's why everyone is not glued to CNN like we were in the Pentagon," said Chuck. "Now I can watch the Wizards and Caps and . . ."

"Not so fast Chuck," Mary interrupted. "There's plenty for us to do."

"Okay, but how does Otto contact Rick, Mr. Pickard, and the others?"

"Instant messaging and email were steps forward in the 1990s, but now Otto has made the alerting process faster and more reliable. Otto keeps track of the Sit Room director, the national security adviser, his deputy, all of the NSC staff, some senior White House staff members, and the President. Otto knows their location by noting what device they are using. If Mr. Pickard is on his desktop computer, then Otto sends my alert to his screen. If he is on his WHCA phone at home, Otto sends my message to that line. If Mr. Pickard is not actively using a device, then Otto sends the alert to his default device, most likely his Shazaam, the combination cell phone and PDA that everyone in the White House carries. If Mr. Pickard is meeting with the President, he sets his Shazaam to Tickle instead of Tone."

"How does Crisis Brief work?" asked Chuck.

"Prior to the terrorist attacks in 2001, a database common to every agency was an unimaginable concept. Agencies did not trust each other to protect sensitive information, much less understand it. A former NSC executive secretary once said that agencies classified only 10 percent of information to protect sensitive data, sources, and methods. They classified the rest to keep other agencies away from the information.

"But 9-11 forced better interagency sharing of data. Prior to that, no agency, say CIA, wanted to let another, FBI, as an example, troll through CIA databases looking for linkages to FBI leads, or vice versa. Many felt that the FBI had forewarning information about the 9-11 hijackings, but it was never integrated with related foreign intelligence at CIA. Intelink was an improvement in the intelligence community, but the agencies only posted finished product on that system. Gradually, the bosses pressured each organization, including law enforcement agencies, to add more information. The size and value of the common pool of data grew as each agency gained confidence in the security constraints that controlled access to the data. Crisis Net and Crisis Brief were built on that common database and were outgrowths of Intelink.

"Sure, some data are never added to the common database—each agency holds back its family jewels. But a special coordinating committee works potential links between the interagency 'jewels.' During crises, the threshold governing what data are fed to the pool goes up, allowing the sharing of critical information. The security people use biometric authentication—iris scans, handprints, and such—to control access to the common data. Also, Crisis Net's voice recognition software constantly monitors every teleconference to ensure that no unauthorized participant joins the group."

"Is this approach working?" asked Chuck.

"The computer system works well, but there are lingering institutional biases and cultural hang-ups at each agency that hinder complete integration. In fact, just last month, CIA started moaning when . . ."

"Mary, the Note is ready."

Mary accessed the Note that Norm had just finished. He had written a one-page summary of the situation and included two pointers at the bottom. One was to the CIA report. The second was to the Crisis Brief page that Otto had set up with information from the History file on recent reporting of both recent events in Tropicland and a previous coup in 1993. If either Mr. Pickard or Stephanie wanted more information, they could access the NSC network, log on to Crisis Brief, and read the available background material. Mary double-checked the distribution list, noting that Otto had added the Vice President's national security adviser to the recipient list she had given him. "I always forget that guy," Mary muttered.

"What's that?" asked Norm.

"Nothing. The note looks great. Post it. All right, let's see if we can find out what Colonel Badguy is up to."

= = =

"Hey, Mary, CNN's got Colonel Badguy giving a speech at Government House."

A week after Colonel Badguy had proven CIA right by staging a successful coup against President Goodguy, Mary, Norm, and Chuck were on their first day shift. After Badguy had forced Goodguy into exile in Miami, Badguy had seized control of the army, purged Goodguy's cabinet, and destroyed the country's only independent TV station. U.S. President John Haynes had met with his national security team via video conference following the coup, and Rick White had told the duty officers the group agreed that Americans in Tropicland should be warned of the unstable situation. White had also said that State would send a special envoy to Palmville, who, along with the U.S. Ambassador who knew Colonel Badguy well, would attempt to meet with the colonel and determine his next steps.

Today, Badguy spoke to his supporters from the colonnaded front of the seat of government. Both CNN and Otto were translating Badguy's speech into English.

"Badguy is threatening to take American citizens in Tropicland hostage," Norm told Mary as she and Chuck watched the video on their workstations. The Sit Room had added video streaming to the NSC network in 2001, but Otto made the whole process easier.

Donning her headset, Mary addressed the computer. "Otto, initiate a Crisis Net video conference with the standard attendees.

"Norm, send an alert to Stephanie Smith and ask her to either log onto the Crisis Net meeting on her desktop or come over here and join us. I will tell Rick what's up." Mary turned to Chuck and explained to him that possible hostage taking by Badguy would escalate the situation in Tropicland, and Smith, the NSC staffer who handled Tropicland matters, needed to be in the loop to help determine the depth of the potential problem. Smith had an office across West Exec in the Eisenhower EOB and she could pick up not only the CNN feed on her desktop computer, but also the impending Crisis Net video conference. Or she could join the meeting the old-fashioned way and walk across the street to the Sit Room. Mary then walked into Rick White's office, the director of the Sit Room, briefed him on the new development in Tropicland, and told him about the pending Crisis Net conference.

Just then, Otto opened Mary's Alert window on her workstation and flashed the message: "Tropicland filter hit. See Crisis Net/Tropicland/coup/resort."

Sitting down at her workstation, she clicked on the pointer and read a new report from the State Department that described how Badguy's henchmen had stormed the Twin Palms Hotel and Spa earlier that day, rousted all the guests, and left them on the highway with their luggage. Badguy's men posted armed guards at the entrance to the seaside resort and chased away a freelance reporter and cameraman. As she read the cable, Otto flashed another alert. The freelancer must have been pretty quick on his feet, because MSNBC began rolling his video of the stranded tourists in front of the Twin Palms.

Norm was well into the Crisis Net meeting when Mary

joined the group. Stephanie Smith arrived in the Sit Room just as Mary addressed the other duty officers. Stephanie and Rick White stood behind Mary, just out of the field of view of the video camera atop her workstation.

"What does everyone think about the Twin Palms deal?" Mary asked. No one had any theories about the development, except for the wise-ass NSA duty officer who suggested that Badguy's parents might be visiting and, despite the coup, sea-side rooms were scarce.

While Norm alerted Mr. Pickard and others to Colonel Bad-guy's speech, Smith asked Mary to help her set up a video tele-conference of the Action Committee. Its members were at the assistant secretary level in each agency; Smith gave Mary the list of people he wanted included.

"Chuck, watch how John (the team's comms technician) sets up this conference for Stephanie," Mary said. "Use the back room because Bennett has a meeting in the front room at 3:00 P.M. and we don't want to disturb him." Chuck, still heavy into the learning mode, asked Stephanie the purpose of the meeting.

"I want the group to exchange views on these developments in Tropicland and discuss whether the U.S. should change the position we took after the coup. If Badguy intends to take Americans hostage, we might want to consider intervention, or at least evacuation."

Mary turned to Kevin Issacson, the day shift analyst who was drafting the Sit Room's Evening Summary, and reminded him to check Otto's Multilog for the minutes of the Crisis Net ses-sion. "Also, please talk to Stephanie when she finishes her meeting to see if she has any additions about your write-up on the Tropicland situation."

Almost an hour later, Smith emerged from her virtual meet-ing with the Action Committee. She told Rick and Mary that the group had decided to ask for increased overhead coverage of Tropicland and enhanced reporting from NSA. Also, CIA was to see if their sources could give warning of kidnapping plans and the Assistant Secretary of State would propose that the Palmville embassy urge AmCits (American citizens) to leave the country.

"Ask Otto to send the meeting transcript to me. I will brief Pickard and Bennett on my meeting with the Action session," Smith said to Rick, "but please watch for the results of the increased intelligence collection. Watch the demonstrators in the streets, not just Badguy's people. Remember, in 1979, the 'students' did the dirty work for the Iranian mullahs when they seized our embassy in Tehran."

=== === ===

Two days later, Otto alerted Mary's team that NIMA, the National Imagery and Mapping Agency, had issued an imagery highlight report on an unusual construction project at the Twin Palms.

Chuck read the report with newfound skills: "NIMA says that a fence is under construction around the Twin Palms resort. The fence is about half completed."

"Click on the attachment and bring up the imagery," instructed Mary. As they looked at the satellite imagery, Norm mused aloud, "Why are they building a fence around a hotel?"

Mary stepped into Rick White's office and briefed him on the fence going up around the Twin Palms hotel.

"Mary, I think Colonel Badguy is building himself a hostage compound," said White. "Pickard is at a meeting at the Pentagon. You alert him and Stephanie Smith. I will go upstairs and tell Bennett."

"Norm, start a Crisis Net conference," Mary said. "Find out if anyone has anything on the Twin Palms construction, Badguy's plans, and how many AmCits are left in Tropicland. Oh, and Chuck, alert the VP's guy."

"Otto, alert Daniel Pickard and Stephanie Smith. My message is: "Overhead imagery today shows a fence under construction at Twin Palms, the resort that Badguy seized on Wednesday. Rick White thinks that Colonel Badguy could turn the hotel into a hostage compound. We are looking for further information. Mary Simmons, SDO."

Pickard was in his car as it crossed the Potomac toward the District when he got Mary's alert on his Shazaam. He called Mary on the Shazaam secure line and she explained that she had no additional information, but that Jim Bennett had just entered the Sit Room and was setting up a Deputies Committee meeting on the secure video teleconferencing system.

"Where's the President?" Pickard asked. Mary looked at a small window in the upper-right corner of her workstation screen and said, "Oval Office."

"I'll call him, but if he wants details, what do you have that he can read?"

"When he opens Crisis Brief, Otto will know it's the President and will direct him to a three-level page that has buttons for an executive summary of everything we know, a broader, working-level compendium, and last, the raw reports," Mary said.

Later, as Mary and her team prepared to turn over with the oncoming night watch, she opened a page where Otto recorded presidential browsing. She smiled to herself when she saw that he had opened most everything that Crisis Brief had on the Tropicland page, even reading a few of the working-level reports from NSA and CIA. She also saw the familiar red flag that indicated Otto prohibited her from seeing the log of other queries and entries made by the President. Otto denied access to some people, even the senior duty officer in the White House Situation Room. "Oh well," she thought. "I guess I don't need to know."

= = =

"Mary, the President will be making several phone calls today," said Situation Room director Rick White. "The first will be at 11:00 this morning to Mexican President Ramirez. Also, Bennett told me that the President might have a NSC meeting late this afternoon in the conference room, so check the room carefully. FYI, the Principals Committee met last night after you went off watch, but Bennett is not sure what they will recommend we do about Tropicland."

This was the last day shift for Mary's team, and even though they were looking forward to a few days off, they knew they were in for a long shift before that break.

"Norm, you take care of the precall routine for Mexico. Chuck, please watch how Norm does this, but keep a look out for anything new on Tropicland as we get close to 11:00." Mary said. "I'll get everyone some coffee."

Norm instructed Otto to "Dial Mexico." The computer checked the Head of State database, found the telephone contact for the president of Mexico, activated a modem, and dialed the specified number. A window opened on Norm's screen and displayed the contact's name and title and the local time in Mexico City.

"This is the White House Situation Room in Washington calling," said Norm. "President Haynes wants to speak with President Ramirez at 11:00 A.M., Washington time, today. Will President Ramirez be available?"

"Yes," replied Ramirez's assistant. "Our embassy in Washington just notified me of the proposed telephone call. I will await your call at 10:45."

"Thanks and good day," Norm said and hung up. "Otto, call Stephanie Smith."

Otto found Stephanie logged onto the NSC network at her desk, dialed her extension, and connected her to Norm's console.

"Good morning, Stephanie. It's Norm in the Sit Room. I

presume you already know, but the President is calling Ramirez at 11:00."

"Yes," Smith replied. "I posted the President's talking points on Brief. You will patch me into the call, right?"

"You bet. Talk to you later."

"Why do we need the President's talking points?" Chuck asked Norm.

"They help us follow the conversation," Norm said. "Before Otto, duty officers took verbatim notes of the call, so the talking points were more important then. Also, the interpreter from State used them to help in the translation. Now, Otto not only translates if the other head of state doesn't speak English, but also converts the dialogue to text. And he creates a record of the call so we don't have to produce a Memorandum of Conversation. We listen in just in case there is a glitch."

$$=\ =\ =$$

"Okay, folks. Are we ready for the NSC meeting?" Rick White inspected the entry foyer, the front conference room, and even the duty officer area. Sometimes the President stopped by after a meeting to say howdy to the Sit Room staff, so White didn't want any leftovers from lunch in sight.

"Why is the President coming down here instead of video conferencing from the Oval Office like he usually does?" asked Chuck.

"He seems comfortable with the video link except when American lives might be at stake and he has to make hard decisions," said White. "Then, Haynes wants to look his people in the eye and read their body language."

"That must mean we are sending troops to Tropicland," said Chuck. "Do you know what's up?"

"Bennett told me last night that the Principals were leaning toward intervention, but they plan to present the President with several options today. We'll just have wait and see."

White turned away from Chuck and greeted the Secretaries

of State and Defense as they walked into the conference room. The DCI, Chairman, Attorney General, and John Haynes' closest political adviser soon followed. Stephanie Smith was there, too. Mary moved around to the steps leading down from the NSC Secretariat and saw a Secret Service agent leading the way for the President. Haynes, followed by his chief of staff and Dan Pickard, walked briskly into the conference room, leaving two Secret Service agents at the door. Mary closed the door that separated the conference room from the duty officers' stations and switched on the warning lights above each door to the conference room.

Chuck was screening information on the Internet, Norm was working with Kevin Issacson on the Evening Summary, and Mary was watching CNN when Stephanie Smith opened the door to the conference room. She whispered, "The President wants to see the video of Badguy's speech, the one where he threatens to take AmCits hostage."

"Otto, retrieve Colonel Badguy's speech from the Tropicland page in Crisis Brief," Mary said into her headset mike. "Roll it immediately in the front conference room and my workstation." Fifteen seconds later, Stephanie gave Mary a thumbs-up and closed the door.

"Does that happen very often?" asked Chuck.

"Occasionally," said Mary. "Rick told me that Haynes is almost like Kennedy. If he thinks an answer to his question is too general, he drills down for the details. Maybe he wants to see Badguy for himself, rather than just read the speech text."

Just minutes after the tape ended, Smith opened the door again. "Get our Ambassador in Palmville on a videophone for the President."

Mary instructed Otto to dial the embassy. "I hope the guy is still at work," Mary said to Norm. A receptionist answered the phone at the embassy and indeed the Ambassador was available. "Have him call the Situation Room on your videophone,"

Mary instructed, giving the receptionist the number for WHCA's video telephone switchboard. "Norm, tell WHCA to patch his call to the NSC net. Chuck, slip Stephanie a note that the Ambassador will be on the line shortly."

After several anxious minutes, Ambassador Upton appeared on Mary's screen. "Good afternoon, Mr. Ambassador. I am Mary Simmons, Situation Room duty officer. Do you read me loud and clear?"

"I do indeed, and good afternoon to you."

"One moment for the President," Mary said. She pulled down the video streaming menu on her screen and clicked "Patch," then "Front Conference Room." When she saw Stephanie wave and close the door, Mary knew she had a good connection for the President.

"Wow," said Chuck. "That was slick. Tell me how . . ."

The alert bell rang on Norm's workstation, interrupting Chuck's question. A window opened on his screen and flashed: "Tropicland filter hit. See Crisis Net/Tropicland/coup/resort/fence."

Norm opened the file. "NIMA says that the fence around the Twin Palms is complete, and there are military vehicles inside the compound. Here's a copy of the report."

Mary took the report next door to Rick White who quickly read it. "Mary, be ready to send the imagery to the conference room." Rick opened the door to the conference room, eliciting an angry glare from the chief of staff. Rick smiled back and handed the report to Stephanie who was sitting against the wall behind Dan Pickard. Stephanie read it while Rick waited, then gave it to Pickard, who also quickly saw the significance of the report.

"Mr. President," Pickard said as he looked across the table. "We are running out of time."

= = =

Several days later, when Mary, Norm, and Chuck were starting the first of another string of night watches, elements of the

101st Airborne Division had stabilized the situation in Tropicland. The infantry had parachuted into Palmville, carrying out President Haynes's threat of U.S. intervention. They reported only minor skirmishes with Badguy's forces; the mere presence of U.S. troops had seemed to convince Badguy himself to decamp for the inland mountains, leaving behind only token resistance. President Goodguy, bolstered by not only U.S. forces, but also strong support from the United Nations and the Organization of American States, regained the position to which he had been elected two years before.

It was about 10:00 in the evening. Norm was upstairs closing up Dan Pickard's office after the national security adviser left for home. Mary was in the ladies room when one of the White House switchboard lines rang on Chuck's phone console.

"The President is calling. Who is speaking, please?" said the operator.

"This is Chuck, ah, Chuck Holmes," he said, frantically looking around for Mary.

"Thank you. One moment for the President."

Mary told him to always be ready to answer a "What's new?" question from upstairs, especially the President. "Keep the latest cable or intelligence report handy, just in case someone calls," she said. But he had not. What should he say to the President?

"Good evening, Chuck. This is the President. What's new in Tropicland?"

"Well, ah, sir, it has been, ah, pretty quiet," Chuck said, wincing at his lame response. He was opening Crisis Brief when the President came on the line, so he clicked on the Update button on the Tropicland page. Much to his relief, the crisis filter had just caught a situation report from the commander-in-chief, Southern Command.

"Just a second, Mr. President. Otto just received a Situation Report from the Joint Forces Command. They report that there have been no engagements in the past six hours. The commander on the ground said that only a few dozen of Colonel Badguy's men remain at large. President Goodguy remains at Government House."

"Thanks Chuck. Good report. But one question."

"Yes sir. What's that?"

"Who's Otto?"

APPENDIX

Presidents, National Security Advisers, and Situation Room Directors, 1961–2002

President	National Security Adviser	Director
John F. Kennedy	McGeorge Bundy	Gerry McCabe
		Oliver Hallett
Lyndon B. Johnson	McGeorge Bundy	Art McCafferty
	Walter Rostow	
Richard M. Nixon	Henry Kissinger	David McManis
		Jim Fazio
Gerald R. Ford	Henry Kissinger	Jim Fazio
	Brent Scowcroft	
Jimmy Carter	Zbigniew Brzezinski	Dennis Chapman
Ronald Reagan	Richard Allen	Manny Rubio
	William Clark	Michael Bohn
	Robert McFarlane	Paul LeBras
	John Poindexter	Neil O'Leary
	Frank Carlucci	
	Colin Powell	
George H. W. Bush	Brent Scowcroft	Neil O'Leary
William Clinton	Tony Lake	Neil O'Leary
	Sandy Berger	Jim Reed
		Joyce Harmon
		Kevin Cosgriff
		Elliot Powell
George W. Bush	Condoleeza Rice	Elliot Powell
		Deborah Loewer

BIBLIOGRAPHY

Books

Aaron, David. *State Scarlet*. New York: Putnam, 1987.

Andrew, Christopher. *For the President's Eyes Only*. New York: HarperCollins, 1995.

Berman, Larry. *Lyndon Johnson's War*. New York: Norton, 1989.

Brugioni, Dino A. *Eyeball to Eyeball*. New York: Random House, 1991.

Clancy, Tom. *The Bear and the Dragon*. New York: G. Putnam's Sons, 2000.

Destler, I. M., Leslie Gelb, and Anthony Lake. *Our Own Worst Enemy*. New York: Simon & Schuster, 1984.

Ford, Gerald R. *A Time to Heal*. New York: Harper and Row, 1979.

Gates, Robert M. *From the Shadows*. New York: Simon & Schuster, 1996.

Goodwin, Doris Kearns. *Lyndon Johnson and the American Dream*. New York: Harper, 1976.

Hersh, Seymour. *The Dark Side of Camelot*. New York: Little, Brown, 1997.

Johnson, Lyndon. *The Vantage Point*. New York: Holt, 1971.

Jordan, Hamilton. *Crisis*. New York: Berkley, 1983.

Kissinger, Henry A. *White House Years*. New York: Little, Brown, 1979.

Lake, Anthony. *6 Nightmares*. Boston: Little, Brown, 2000.

Legere, L. J., and Kenneth Clark, eds. *The President and the Management of National Security*. New York: Praeger, 1969.

Neuman, Johanna. *Lights, Camera, War*. New York: St. Martin's Press, 1996.

Oberdorfer, Don. *Tet!* Garden City, N.Y: Doubleday, 1971.

Prados, John. *Keepers of the Keys.* New York: Morrow, 1991.

Reeves, Richard. *President Kennedy: Profile of Power.* New York: Simon & Schuster, 1993.

Scheslinger, Arthur M. *A Thousand Days.* New York: Houghton Mifflin, 1965.

Sick, Gary. *All Fall Down: America's Tragic Encounter with Iran.* New York: Random House, 1985.

————. *October Surprise: American Hostages in Iran and the Election of Ronald Reagan.* New York: Times Books, 1991.

Sorensen, Theodore C. *Kennedy.* New York: Harper and Row, 1965.

Wetterhahn, Ralph. *The Last Battle.* New York: Carroll & Graf, 2001.

Wyden, Peter. *Bay of Pigs: The Untold Story.* New York: Simon & Schuster, 1979.

Journal, Newspaper, and Internet Articles

Allen, Richard V. "The Day Reagan was Shot." *Atlantic Monthly*, April 2001.

Anderson, Jack. "When the President Hits the Road." *Parade*, June 11, 1967.

Barry, John. "Our Target Was Terror." *Newsweek*, August 31, 1998.

Bedard, Paul, et al. "Mustn't See TV." *U.S. News & World Report*, July 23, 2001.

Bennet, James. "Targeting Terrorism." *Houston Chronicle*, August 22, 1998.

"Clinton Denies Knowledge of Funding Abuse." Associated Press. St. Louis Post-Dispatch, July 25, 2000.

Cole, Kenneth. "Embassy Bomb Victims Make Final Journey Home." Detroit Press, August 14, 1998.

Deans, Bob. "Businesslike Bush War Council Lacks Movie Drama." *Atlanta Journal Constitution*, October 28, 2001.

Dickerson, John. "Inside the War Room." *Time*, December 31, 2001.

Donley, Michael, Cornelius O'Leary, and John Montgomery. "Inside the White House Situation Room." www.odci.gov/csi/studies, *Studies in Intelligence*. Vol. 1, no. 1, 1997.

Drew, Christopher. "After 30 Years, The Hot Line to Cool Off the Cold War Is Still On Call." *Austin American-Statesman*, August 15, 1993.

Elsey, George M. "Blueprints for Victory." *National Geographic Magazine*, May 1995.

Ginor, Isabella. "How the Six Day War Almost Led to Armageddon." *Guardian*, June 10, 2000.

Grunwald, Michael. "U.S. Complaint Links Bin Laden to Bombing." *Washington Post*, August 29, 1998.

Hackworth, David H., "Hell in a Handbasket." *Maxim*, January 2001.

Healy, Melissa. "The Washington Summit Treaty is Ready—but Centers on Risk Reduction Are Not." *Los Angeles Times*, December 11, 1987.

Hoffman, David. "Shattered Shield." *Washington Post*, March 15, 1998.

"How Johnson Brings the World to His Desk." *Business Week*, March 4, 1967.

Isikoff, Michael. "A Pardon Overheard." *Newsweek*, August 27, 2001.

Kelly, Jack. "2 Held in Embassy Bombings; More Arrests Likely." *USA Today*, August 20, 1998.

Lacey, Marc, "Clinton Spoofs Himself as Lame Duck." *New York Times*, May 1, 2000.

LaFraniere, Sharon, John Pomfret, and Lena Sun. "Riadys' Persistent Pursuit of Influence." *Washington Post*, May 27, 1997.

McNulty, Timothy, "Decisions at the Speed of Light." *Chicago Tribune*, December 22, 1991.

Naughton, James, "On Watch in the White House Basement for Armageddon." *New York Times*, May 10, 1977.

Nowrasteh, Cyrus, "Counter Punch: Filmmaker Holds Firm on Reagan Movie's Accuracy." *Los Angeles Times*, December 24, 2001.

Paige, Emmett, Jr. "The Rapid Expansion of Intelink." www.DefenseLink.mil/speeches. Vol. 11, no. 66.

"Pakistan Arrests 2 More in Embassy Bombings." *Houston Chronicle*, August 19, 1998.

Pincus, Walter. "A Tempting Site for Spies' Eyes." *Washington Post*, September 3, 2001.

————. "PDB, the Only News Not Fit for Anyone Else to Read." *Washington Post*, August 27, 1994.

"Potent, Not Omnipotent, Even in the US, the President Is Fettered." *Guardian*, January, 15, 2000.

Raum, Tom. "US, Russia Stress Communication, A New Moscow-Russia Hot Line." *Boston Globe*, July 27, 1999.

Reston, James. "U.S. Hot Line to Soviet: Little Use for 20 Years." *New York Times*, April 5, 1983.

Risen, James, "On Economic Matters, Man to See is Clinton Aide Rubin." *Los Angeles Times*, February 10, 1993.

Rust, Michael. "Caught on Tape." *Washington Times*, December 13, 1999.

Sauer, Jeff. "White House Puts the 'W' in Video." *Emedia Magazine*, May 2001.

Schulman, Bruce J. "Taping History." *Journal of American History*, September 1998.

Simon, Roger, and Bob Kemper. "Africa Tragedy Curtails Clinton Fundraising Tour." *Chicago Tribune*, August 11, 1998.

Stone, Webster. "Moscow's Still Holding." *New York Times Magazine*, September 8, 1988.

"U.S.-Soviet Hot Line." *Wall Street Journal*, November 19, 1985.

VandeHei, Jim. "President's New Life Has an International Focus." *Wall Street Journal*, September 27, 2001.

Waller, Douglas. "The Sit-Room Waiting List." *Time*, November 26, 2001.

Woodward, Bob. "White House Taping System Disclosed." *Washington Post*, December 19, 1986.

Unpublished Material

Speeches

Beal, Richard S. "Decision Making, Crisis management, Information Technology." Seminar on Intelligence and Command and Control, spring 1984, Harvard University, Program for Information Resources Policy.

Lucas, James W. "The Information Needs of Presidents." Seminar on Intelligence and Command and Control, spring 1990, Harvard University, Program for Information Resources Policy.

McDaniel, Rodney B. "C3I: A National Security Council Perspective." Seminar on Intelligence and Command and Control, spring 1987, Harvard University, Program for Information Resources Policy.

Research Papers

Radi, David A. "Intelligence Inside the White House." Program for Information Policy, Harvard University, March 1997.

Interviews with the author, January–December, 2001

Bator, Francis
Benn, Allen
Botsai, Sally
Bradshaw, Terry
Bush, George H. W.
Campanella, Tony
Chapman, Dennis
Clift, A. Denis
Cosgriff, Kevin
Cramer, Michael
Crowley, P. J.
Enright, Michael
Enright, Sean
Fazio, Jim
Ford, Gerald R.
Fuerth, Leon
Gantt, Florence
Gates, Robert
Glick, Bonnie
Goodpaster, Andrew
Haass, Richard

Haig, Alexander
Hardy, Ken
Howe, Johnathan
Kay, Gilda
Kaysen, Carl
Kimmitt, Robert
Kissinger, Henry
Lake, Anthony
LeBras, Paul
Leshin, Marty
Levine, Sol
McCabe, Joy Dell
McDaniel, Rodney
McFarlane, Robert
McManus, David
McNamara, Robert
O'Connell, Kevin
O'Hara, Robert
O'Hara, Rosanne
O'Leary, Neil
Odom, William
Poindexter, John
Popadiuk, Roman
Powell, Elliot
Radi, David
Reishus, Sharon
Rostow, Walter
Saunders, Harold
Schecter, Jerrold
Scowcroft, Brent
Sedney, David
Sesno, Frank
Shepard, Tazewell
Shergalis, Joe
Sick, Gary

Sims, Robert
Smith, Gayle
Sorensen, Theodore
Steinberg, James
Studeman, William
Sullivan, Stephanie
Wergeles, Fred

Private Collections

Enright, Charles. "Recollections of the Situation Room." November 21, 1986. Courtesy of Sean Enright.

Kissinger, Henry A. Letter to V. James Fazio, January 15, 1977. Courtesy of Jim Fazio.

———. "Memorandum for the President." February 10, 1969. Courtesy of David Y. McManis.

———. "Memorandum for the President." March 18, 1969. Courtesy of David Y. McManis.

McManis, David Y. "The White House Situation Room." July 23, 1973.

Public Documents

Fisher-Thompson, Jim. "President Clinton Addresses Burundi Peace Talks Participants." The Washington File, U.S. State Department.

Smith, Bromley K. "Organizational History of the National Security Council During the Kennedy and Johnson Administrations," Executive Secretary of the NSC, September 1, 1988.

Weekly Compilation of Presidential Documents; Remarks on departure for Washington, D.C., from Martha's Vineyard, Massachusetts; Washington, August 24, 1998.

"White House Communications Agency." Undated fact sheet from Defense Information Systems Agency.

Unpublished Material, National Archives, Presidential Papers

Harry S Truman Library, Independence, Missouri

Oral History. George Elsey, February 10, 1964.

John F. Kennedy Library, Boston, Massachusetts

Memorandum for J. M. Leftis, International Situation Room, staffing of. Kenneth O'Donnell, February 21, 1963.

Memorandum for McGeorge Bundy, Night Log. L. J. Legere, October 31, 1962.

Memorandum for McGeorge Bundy, Night Log. M. V. Forrestal, October 24, 1962.

Memorandum for the President, Cold War Control Center. Godfrey T. McHugh, April 25, 1961.

Memorandum for the President, Current Organization of the White House and NSC for Dealing with International Matters. McGeorge Bundy, June 22, 1961.

Memorandum to John McCone, Charles Enright. McGeorge Bundy, November 13, 1962.

Memorandum to Kenneth O'Donnell, NSC Office Space. McGeorge Bundy, January 5, 1962.

Memorandum to the President, White House Organization. McGeorge Bundy, May 16, 1961.

NSC Record of Actions, Standing Group Meeting. Bromley Smith, January, 5, 1962.

Oral history. Bromley Smith, July 16, 1970.

Situation Room Summary, April 2, 1963.

Lyndon B. Johnson Library, Austin, Texas

Lyndon Johnson Daily Diary, June 6 and June 10, 1967.

Memorandum for Bromley Smith, Situation Room Personnel. Art McCafferty, June 3, 1963.

Memorandum for Bromley Smith, Space Requirements for Communications Support of the Situation Room. Art McCafferty, July 1, 1965.

Memorandum for General Wheeler, Situation Room Communications with MAC-V. W.W. Rostow, January 30, 1968.

Memorandum for Joseph Califano, Situation Room Staffing. McGeorge Bundy, October 16, 1964.

Memorandum for Leo Bourassa, Notifications. Art McCafferty, May 3, 1966.

Memorandum for McGeorge Bundy, Documents and Reports Sent to the President. Bromley Smith, October 6, 1965.

Memorandum for the President, Christmas Greeting from Soviet Hot Line Technicians. W. W. Rostow, December 28, 1968.

Memorandum for the President, Military Situation in South Viet Nam for the Week 24–30 October, 1965. Situation Room Briefing Officer, November 2, 1965.

Memorandum for the Record, Khe Sanh Relief Map. Art McCafferty, May 21, 1968.

Memorandum for the Record, Walt Rostow's Recollections of June 5, 1967. Harold Saunders, November 17, 1968.

Memorandum for the Situation Room. Art McCafferty, May 25, 1966.

Memorandum for the Situation Room, Laudatory Comments from Secretary McNamara. Art McCafferty, June 9, 1967.

Memorandum for the Situation Room, Operational Procedures. Art McCafferty, May 25, 1966.

Memorandum for the White House Situation Room, Notifications. James U. Cross, June 2, 1966.

Memorandum for W. Marvin Watson, Construction of Shielded Communications Enclosure in the Situation Room. Roy S. Eckert, August 17, 1965.

Memorandum of Conversation, The Hot Line Exchanges. Nathaniel Davis, November 4, 1968.

Note to the President, Draft Fact DoD Fact Sheet on Washington-Moscow Hot Line. George Reedy, March 27, 1965.

Oral History. Robert McNamara, undated.

Oral History. Bess Abell, July 1, 1969.

Oral History. Bromley K. Smith, July 29, 1969.
Washington-Moscow "Hot-Line" Exchange, NSC History, Mid East
    Crisis, vol. 7.

Richard M. Nixon Collection, National Archives,
Washington, D.C.

Memorandum for the Record, Interview with General V. Clifton. Dr.
    L. J. Legere and Dick Moose, July 29, 1968.

Press Releases and Audiovisual Material

Press Releases

"White House Selects VBrick to deliver Real-time Video over IP."
    VBrick Systems, February 27, 2001.

Radio and Television

The Diane Rehm Show. National Public Radio, August 10, 2001.
"National Security Council." *Washington Journal.* C-SPAN, Septem-
    ber 17, 1997.

Audio Recordings

Recordings and Transcripts of Telephone Conversations, Situation
    Room Series. Lyndon B. Johnson Presidential Library.

Audiovisual Briefings

"Project Genoa," Defense Advanced Research Projects Agency, un-
    dated.

INDEX

The author, with President and Mrs. Nixon, was a social aide to Nixon in the early 1970s. *White House Photo*

The author and George H. W. Bush. *White House Photo*

ABOUT THE AUTHOR

MICHAEL BOHN graduated from Texas Tech in 1965 with a bachelor of arts in government and received a master of arts, also in government, two years later. An intelligence officer in the Navy during the period 1969–88, Bohn served in Vietnam, aboard ships at sea, and at intelligence centers ashore. During 1984–85, he was a senior fellow at the Atlantic Council in Washington, D.C. Bohn was a military social aide to President Richard M. Nixon and director of the White House Situation Room under President Ronald Reagan. After retiring from the Navy, Bohn was a program manager for the consulting firm Booz Allen & Hamilton. He now lives and writes in Alexandria, Virginia.

President Reagan and the Bohn family.